Saved, Sanctified, and Addicted to Porn

Saved, Sanctified, and Addicted to Porn

Overcoming Sexual Perversion

D'onte J. Carroll, Sr.

Kingdom Living Publishing
Accokeek, MD

Kingdom Living Publishing
P.O. Box 660
Accokeek, MD 20607

Reach us on the Internet: www.kingdomlivingbooks.com
Reach us by phone: (301)292-9010

Published in the United States of America. For worldwide distribution.

ISBN 978-0-9799798-7-3

Acknowledgments

First and foremost, I want to thank God for delivering me and getting me to a place where I can freely talk about this experience. I thank Him for giving me the tools, the outline He gave me for this book, and His timing and strategic planning. I want to thank my family and my kids, D'onte Jr. and Nigel, for being an inspiration to keep pressing forward in difficult times.

I want to thank LaMika for one conversation that sparked up my interest in finishing this book and just being a good friend throughout one of the most difficult times in my life. I want to thank my coworkers in the Southeast Field Unit who have always been a strong support system and have encouraged me to finish this book so they can read what God has placed on my heart.

To all of those struggling with an addiction of any kind, this book is for you!

Contents

Introduction

I want to thank every reader that has decided to grace their eyes upon this book. In this book, I will be focusing on an addiction to pornography or porn, which I struggled with for many years. The porn industry is one of the top successful industries in the nation. Web sites draw millions of visitors daily. Various statistics show the porn industry generates revenue of a minimum of 3 billion dollars a year. Porn is a lucrative industry. Why would it not be? "Sex sells" is not just a cliché, it is the truth. Quite often, we hear and know the stories of family members and friends that are substance abusers, addicted to alcohol, shopping, gambling, and many other habits. Yet, we do not hear too often the testimonies of those that are addicted to sex and or pornography and the effect it has on their lives.

In the church, people who are addicted to sex and have a serious addiction to pornography are identified as having a spirit of perversion or a lust spirit on them. I was one of those people. While I was guilty of being addicted to pornography, I tried to free myself. I soon realized that there are no specific programs or institutions geared to help people who are battling an addiction to pornography.

My hope and prayer after you read this book are that a word, sentence, Scripture, analogy, metaphor, or truth I have shared will ignite a fire in you to the point you want to use any influence and power you have to help yourself or someone who is struggling with this addiction. Pornography has broken marriages, families, depleted finances, and destroyed lives, in general. I will be sharing with you moments and facts of my addiction and offering solutions on how to overcome it.

To those who are super-saved in the church, if you are reading this to spectate and find discussion topics for your soap box, allow me to say thank you for helping me to reach the heights that God has for me. If your agenda is to use my story to find fault in me or bring me to the noose to lynch me in the choke hold of condemnation, thank you too!! Guess what, all publicity is good publicity.

Note to reader: As the author gives his true testimony of his addiction to pornography, parts of this book contain language and sexual content that may be unsuitable for young readers and offensive to others. It is the author's hope that the reader will be set free or receive information to aid someone they know who may be addicted.

Chapter 1

What is Pornography?

Pornography (porn), is visual or printed material that depicts deviant sexual behavior, activity or nudity that is designed to entertain or arouse one's hormones to participate in sexual activity whether through masturbation or with a partner. For the most part, pornography is used to bring to life sexual fantasies and or imaginations to help an individual masturbate and experience an orgasm. There are various types of pornography.

First, there is what I call *Hardcore Porn*. In hardcore porn, the sex is graphic and actual intercourse is taking place. Viewers witness real actors having actual sexual intercourse with each other. Filmmakers tend to focus on close-up shots where the audience can see the penetration/intercourse with the actors' genitals; it is raw and in your face! When viewers watch hardcore porn, they will see various sexual positions. Hardcore porn can be found on all the major pornographic sites, late night cable flicks, and in the adult section of video stores usually covered up to hide them from children in generic electronic and video game stores.

Second, there is what I also call *Soft Porn*. Soft porn is what you find in R-rated movies. We refer to them as "sex scenes." Sex scenes in R-rated movies are quite mild and not as graphic. A viewer will see actors kissing, touching inappropriately, and grinding. Unlike porn stars in hardcore porn, the actors in soft porn flicks do not have penetration and or actual sex; they act it out. They wear skin tone pieces to bring the illusion to the camera and its audience as if they are actually nude. In soft porn, one can expect to see a man's chest and a woman's nipples. However, you will almost never see the man or woman's genitals. Viewers will only see enough to get aroused sexually. Even though soft porn creates the illusion that actual sex is taking place, I always felt it had the power to agitate one's imagination and cause them to want to go a step further and look at hardcore porn to entertain a porn addiction or just get quick sexual gratification while masturbating.

Various videos, such as twerk videos, that can be found on social media can fall into the category of soft porn. Twerk videos are videos of women who have curvaceous, voluptuous shapes who the majority of the time wear "booty shorts," sexy lingerie, or miniskirts. They move their hips and backsides in a gyrating motion. Viewers never really see the females faces just their buttocks. In twerk videos, the female is usually bending over in front of the camera shaking what her momma gave her to arouse male viewers. It is almost as if the woman is giving male viewers a cyber lap dance.

Lastly, there is what I call *literary porn*. Literary porn is books, magazines, or anything you read that describes or depicts sexual activity, behavior, or intercourse that has a strong capability of sexually arousing a reader. In the African American community, we have what we call, "hood books." These books have a lot of drug dealer, gang-banging, exotic dancer, around the way girl characters that always engage in graphic sexual activity. Authors Mary B. Morrison, Omar Tyree, and Zane write books such as these. Of the many authors, Zane's work is categorized as the most sexually graphic of them all. I remember when I was an undergraduate student at Strayer University; I had a few classmates, all women, who acknowledged that they were fans of author Zane. They would always say that after reading a chapter filled with a raunchy, graphic, very descriptive sex scene, it made them either immediately go masturbate or go grab their significant other and have sex because of the arousal that a chapter of her book brought on.

Masturbation and pornography go hand in hand. Masturbation is when a man or woman pleases himself or herself sexually to reach an orgasm. The individual uses their hands or sex toys to stimulate themselves sexually to an erotic state to reach an orgasm. Although you do not necessarily need porn to masturbate, many individuals use it to aid in the illusion of a 4-dimensional cognitive sexual experience. The 4-dimensional cognitive sexual experience brings to life the imagination of sexual encounters one may have while masturbating. Simply put, when one conjures up thoughts of having sex with a person while masturbating, the masturbation can help the thoughts and imagination feel real as if the mental encounters are actually happening. Just like any other drug or habit, masturbation and the desire to watch pornography are addictive.

The connection between pornography and masturbation is quite simple. When an individual uses their hands or sex toys to arouse their genitals and fondle themselves, they simultaneously watch the videos to get the 4-dimensional feeling or create and entertain the illusion that they are having intercourse with the actors or with people who perhaps remind them of the actors. It is all about the feeling and imagination. As they fondle themselves through masturbation, addicts can feel and imagine the intercourse. However, in the end, it is just imagination.

Chapter 2

Cause and Effect

Now that we have defined what pornography is and the various kinds of pornographic material available, let us examine the cause and effect of an addiction to pornography. What causes and or leads a person to become addicted to pornography? What effects does the addiction itself have on an addict? There are a plethora of reasons why people become addicted to pornography or for the non-addicts, why they choose to indulge in pornography and masturbation at their leisure. During my ten-year addiction, I found six causes that lead people to have a porn addiction. They are boredom, loneliness, curiosity, low self-esteem, unsatisfied sex life, and depression.

Causes

Boredom

When people are bored, their mind becomes idle, and they brainstorm on ways to entertain themselves. My mother used to say the cliché to me quite often growing up, "An idle mind is the devil's workshop." This statement could not have been more accurate when it comes to idleness being one of the causes of people becoming addicted to pornography. A person who has a lot of spare time on their hands sits in a house all day not being productive and can easily find themselves browsing internet websites or adult cable networks and find enjoyment and gratification from watching pornographic flicks to aid in their masturbation sessions. After all, sex of any kind is pleasurable, whether you are with a partner or by yourself through masturbation. A couple of years into my addiction, I found myself looking at porn and masturbating because I was bored. I was not interested in finding ways to be productive in things that interested me; and lastly, I liked the idea of not getting caught by my mother. Frequent boredom will keep a person entangled in a porn addiction.

Loneliness

Loneliness is another reason a person may resort to having an addiction to pornography. When a person is single or going through a season of solitude, and they find themselves single more often than they are in a relationship, it can be easy for them to become addicted to pornography. The reality that we must not ignore is that people who are lonely have feelings; they have sexual fantasies, sexual desires, and needs. They want to be touched, held and satisfied sexually. The truth is not every individual who is lonely can discipline themselves and save themselves for marriage. Not every lonely person has the same views when it comes to pornography and masturbation.

To a lonely person, pornography and masturbation supplements that void and lack of companionship, partnership, and sex life. People who have given up on love and have accepted the myth that they will always be by themselves tend to be the ones that use porn to cope with their loneliness. For them, acting (moaning, groaning, facial expressions) and staring directly into the camera do something for them. It gives the audience the imagination of someone touching them and being intimate with. The imagination can become 4 dimensional, making it feel all too real. For lonely people, watching pornography and masturbating helps them release all the sexual tension built up inside of them that they wish they could release with a partner.

Curiosity

The third cause of people having a porn addiction is curiosity. For the most part, teenagers and young adults tend to fall into this category. When I was married, my oldest stepson was 13 years old when he was first exposed to pornography. If you are raising teenagers, you will be surprised at how much they have been exposed to and their knowledge when it comes to sex. Listen to the conversations our children are having among themselves in school as early as the 4th grade. Kids these days talk about sex; and they have their phrases and terminology to reference sexual activity, gestures, and behaviors. They grind on each other at parties. Teenage girls are twerking on teenage boys. They are arousing each other sexually and bringing up curiosity in their minds and a desire to want to experience more.

These days, some kids are sexually active believe it or not, before they turn 13 years old. With that in mind, when kids who are not sexually active hear their peers talk about their sexual experiences, pornography, and masturbation, it makes them curious and want to look into either having sex or watching pornography to see exactly what the talk is and what sex is all about. Teenagers face peer pressure and want to fit in and be a part of the cliques and conversations with the popular kids in school. If you do not talk to your children about sex, pornography, and masturbation, you make room for curiosity to have their undivided attention and for them to yield to a willing society that will have no problem exposing them to it all in ways you may not even be ready to handle as a parent. It may bring on an addiction they may not be able to shake.

Low Self-Esteem

The fourth cause that drives people to a porn addiction is low self-esteem. Rejection is deadly to a person's self-esteem. People who have the potential to make an excellent spouse tend to always be the ones to be rejected the most. These are people who have been called ugly, unattractive, fat, overweight, too skinny, too dark, etc. They may not have coke bottle shapes or six packs with broad shoulders, biceps, and triceps of a body builder. However, a lot of times they have good hearts and love very hard. People with low self-esteem, for the most part, have always had their physical appearance constantly talked about in negative ways. Because of it, they tend to hate various things about themselves, often view themselves as unattractive, and despise looking in the mirror. They put less, if any, effort in approaching someone they may find interest in dating or courting, because of the fear of being let down. Therefore, they turn to pornography to partake in an imaginary sexual experience they wish they had.

This group of people tends to believe that no one will ever love them. However, just like anyone else they too have sexual needs, fantasies, and desires. Those with low self-esteem who turn to pornography are a lot of times ashamed and would be embarrassed if anyone found out they had a porn addiction. When I was a kid, I remember when I first learned what masturbation was. I used to say, "Only a person who couldn't get none (sex) masturbates." Boy, was I wrong when I too found myself being a person with low self-esteem. Those with low self-esteem who are heavy into pornography feel like they need pornography because it fills a void. It makes them feel loved, gives them a sense of intimacy they wish they had and feel as though no one will ever give them.

Unsatisfied Sex Life

The fifth cause that leads a person to become addicted to pornography is an unsatisfied sex life. This group of people does not have low self-esteem, nor do they have a hard time getting someone to have sex with them. A lot of times they may even be married. However, whoever they are sexually intimate with may not be doing an excellent job pleasing them sexually the way they would like. Therefore, they turn to pornography to get the gratification and or get their partner to watch with the intent of their partner learning tricks, tips, and techniques to spice up things in the bedroom.

An unsatisfied sex life can and will ruin relationships and marriages. For example, people who have had many sex partners throughout their life can find themselves comparing their current partners to their past partners. For this group of people, they can easily find themselves reminiscing about a previous partner who may have been good in one area of sexual intimacy, while another partner they had was good in another area of sexual intimacy.

Therefore, by the time they settled down and tried to commit to one person and find all the sexual gratification in one spouse, they find it hard because they have had experiences with multiple people. Rather than exploring intimacy with their spouse, they would rather compare their current partner's sexual performance to previous partners. A marriage or relationship can go down the drain because the spouse who is being compared can feel as if they cannot compete with the images and techniques from pornographic flicks or partners from your past who in your mind "turned you out." For this group, an unsatisfied sex life can lead to a person finding simple satisfaction in pornography and masturbation that can lead to an uncontrollable addiction.

Depression

Finally, the last cause that will usher a person to an addiction to pornography is depression. Depression from a bad break up or various life experiences can help a depressed person cope with the heartache one may be feeling. For them, the pornography will help them take their mind off the hurt and pain and temporarily relieve them of the reality of life's problem they simply do not want to face.

Personally, all six of these factors have either caused me to become intrigued to want to continue watching porn after my exposure and or relapse back into an addiction from which I was seeking deliverance.

Effects

While the causes that lead people to turn to pornography and masturbation for temporary amusement and relief seem menial to some, for others, like me, they can lead to being trapped in an addiction that may be quite difficult to be free from. There are some effects an addiction to pornography can have on a person that can be long lasting. These effects are; guilt, despair, damaging one's relationship with God and destroy the individual's personal life.

Guilt

A porn addiction can bring on the effect of guilt, especially for Christians who have a moral and spiritual conscience. Most times we will feel the guilt trip immediately after the gratification from masturbation, and the viewing of the pornographic material is over. The guilt can make you feel as if you are going to hell immediately. The truth of the matter is the addiction can lead you there if you do not make the necessary steps and choices to place the spirit of perversion and lust under subjection to the Spirit and power of God.

A person who feels guilty by way of spiritual and moral convictions will begin to beat themselves up and go crazy mentally. If you are not careful, guilt will keep you bound and prolong your deliverance because you spend more time focusing on the addiction itself rather than seeking help and setting precautions to turn away and stay clean. Guilt brings on what I call self-inflicted condemnation. It is important to keep in mind that God wants us to be free. We allow people and our own criticism to keep us in a state of condemnation; however, the beauty of serving God is that He is a deliverer, redeemer, and purifier all in one. He wants to take the opportunity to forgive us and make us clean, righteous, and holy. However, we have to allow Him the room to make the crooked places straight in our lives. Psalm 103:12 says, *"As far as the east is from the west, so far has He removed our transgressions from us."*

For me, the guilt was always unbearable. Especially as a preacher, people expect me to have every temptation or trick of the enemy mastered with discipline and self-control. The expectation is that I am supposed to be impervious to the trials, tribulations, and struggles of life. However, when your weakness itself is the lack of self-control when it comes to lust, what do you do? How do you handle the guilt, the feeling of being a hypocrite? In actuality, the issue is deeper than hypocrisy; it is a spirit that must be overcome.

Despair

Another effect a person can have from a porn addiction is despair. A porn addict can fall into a pit of despair and find it hard to get out. Especially after a great significant amount of time has gone by and midway into the addiction, the individual begins to notice the repetition and pattern of constant relapsing back into the addiction after multiple attempts to stop and be delivered. I recall feeling as if all hope was lost for me. Being a secret porn addict was my fate, and if I wanted to maintain respect from my peers, I had to keep it a secret from the outside world as much as possible.

It began to feel as if the chance of me becoming free was a fantasy and could not be my reality. The sad part is some individuals will use the despair as an excuse to stay addicted.

Damaged Relationship with God

An addiction to pornography has a spiritual ramification and can ultimately damage one's relationship with God. Isaiah 59:2 says, *"But your iniquities have separated you from your God; and your sins have hidden His face from you so that He will not hear."*

God is a holy God. He requires us to live a life of holiness and to abstain from sexual immorality or perversion. Lust, and pornography fall in the category of sexual perversion. In Romans, chapter one, the Apostle Paul talks about how people ignored God when He called them out of sexual immorality. Men started sleeping with men and women started sleeping with women. Paul goes on to say how their reverence and fear of God was so dim that God turned them loose to their sexual desires, to do and conduct themselves according to what they thought was right. Once He did all hell broke loose for them in every area of their lives. When God makes a decision to let us be, we can wreck our own lives.

When you consistently disobey God, He takes His protection and His hand off you. Then when your life turns upside down, and you come to yourself, you have to backtrack and ask yourself, "Did I do something to bring hell, suffering, and judgment upon myself?" That is why I had to make a decision as it relates to my deliverance. I knew God's will concerning my life and the standard He set, and it was not to be bound by sexual immorality. I understood that required me to walk not just in holiness but freedom and liberty from bondage to be an example of what God can do. I had to run towards deliverance before it was too late.

Destroy an Individual's Personal Life

Lastly, pornography can destroy a person's personal life or life in general. You may be surprised how many people's lives do an 180-degree turn because of this addiction and the lack of resources available for those who are addicted. Every day, especially in various government agencies, someone loses their job because they were caught surfing pornographic websites while on their tour of duty. After receiving a termination notice, the individual has to go home and explain to their families that they no longer have a job and their livelihood is at stake because of a porn addiction they had to entertain while at work.

One can lose focus of their goals and what is important in life because they are spending more time, energy, and sometimes funds feeding an addiction. Therefore, they are neglecting the upkeep of their success in life and endeavors. People spend 10, 20, sometimes 30 years fighting various addictions, not realizing a good portion of their life has been wasted, and they are not able to regain it because they gave in to a habit that they just could not shake.

It is important to keep in mind that every little decision in life matters. So, the next time you are led to entertain your porn addiction, ask yourself if those few moments of pleasure are going to help you achieve your life goals. Will the addiction draw you closer to God and to fulfilling your purpose? Or, is it a distraction? Is your quest to get rid of your boredom and curiosity going to lead you into an addictive state for which you never bargained? Will this put a strain on your marriage? What if your kids find your material; what would it do to them? I beg any and everybody who reads this book and just so happens to gain an interest in pornography to ask yourself these questions and more before you ruin your life. The overall question is will it benefit you; if so how? Paul said in 1 Corinthians 6:12 (NIV), *"I have the right to do anything," you say—but not everything is beneficial. "I have the right to do anything"—but I will not be mastered by anything.* Surely, an addiction to pornography is not beneficial to a person, spiritually or naturally.

Chapter 3

A Seed Planted and a Life Changed

You will never forget some events in life, no matter how tragic, great, life changing, or defining they maybe. As for me, I will never forget the day I was introduced to pornography. On that day the seed was planted, and it changed my life forever.

When I was around the age of about 12 or 13, my mother had a boyfriend. He and I were really close. We talked about everything—girls, life, and issues—I encountered as an adolescent that bothered me. I went to him about things I would never go to my mother about. I was able to confide in him, and I trusted him a great deal. One day I was in my room watching television. I was sitting in a green cookout chair that I had in my room. It was an average day; my mom was at work I believe, and as always, he and I were in the house.

I remember my door was cracked, and he softly knocked on the door. I acknowledged him to come on in. He had his hands behind his back and a grin on his face. At the time I did not understand nor know what was about to happen. Today, I realize that the smile he had was not of him; it was, in fact, a spirit he had entertained, and it was getting ready to pounce on my innocent and vulnerable soul, and I was not equipped to handle it on my own. As I look back and reminisce on that moment, I realized that I was having my own Eve in the Garden of Eden experience where the serpent was tempting me to indulge in an activity that would ultimately change the dynamics of my life forever. I was vulnerable, and the enemy was successful because I was so young and my Adam (my mother) was not there to intercede and intercept the plans and divert the spiritual warfare that was beginning to take place. I do not in any way blame my mother for what happened. God had a plan even in my addiction. Romans 8:28 says, *"And we know that all things work together for good to those who love God, and are called according to His purpose."* The devil's plot consisted of me being bound forever in my addiction. But God had a plan to use my addiction to validate my ministry, authenticate my testimony, to qualify, certify and solidify my walk with Him, and make an example of me that He still delivers and sets free. As ministers of the Gospel, how can we preach and scream to the world that God delivers if we ourselves have never been bound to the point that we needed Him to deliver us?

As he slowly walked into my room with his grin on his face and his hands still behind his back, he asked me a question. *"Dee, we cool?"* I nodded my head with a facial expression painted on my face that said, "Dude that is a no brainer." I responded by saying, "Y*ea we cool.*" He asked me the same question again three more times before I got a bit agitated. In a respectful and lighthearted way, I responded each time by saying, "Y*ea we cool.*" He proceeded to chuckle and smile harder.

Taking his hands from behind his back, he handed me a tape and said, *"Here check this out."* I was anxious and curious to see what was on it. So, I popped it in as he stood at the door and watched. I could tell he had been watching whatever it was himself because it went straight to the action or middle of the scene. I used my remote to press play. Instantly, before my eyes were a man and woman having sex. It was a pornographic tape. For the first time, I saw real penetration, and it looked good; I became aroused immediately. The moans and groans looked real and put images in my head of what it would be like and feel like if I were doing the same things to the woman in the video that the man was doing to her.

I was in awe and excitement. My mom's boyfriend saw how into the flick I was. He said, *"Finish checking it out and get it back to me when you are done."* Then he walked off. Very anxious and eager to get back to the video without distraction I shut my door, and for the next 45 minutes, I watched the entire flick. The porn stars did every sexual position you could think of. I found myself getting an erection which was normal because I got them all the time. At the time, I had seen plenty of late night cable flicks, but nothing was so graphic and real as what I watched that day. This was that "hardcore porn" that I had never seen before. The director and or cameraman had no mercy whatsoever! Showing close up shots of the penetration and genitals seemed like a must.

I found myself constantly repositioning myself in my chair because my manhood was aroused and I did not know what to do. I did not masturbate because I had never done it nor did I know how to do it. Those 45 minutes changed my life. I did not become addicted to pornography right then and there. But, the seed was planted. The addiction did not manifest until months later when once again I was in my room dwelling back on what I witnessed that first time I was exposed to that hardcore porn flick. My mind was idle at the time so much so that I had time to dwell on pornography and how it made me feel. It was at the point where I wanted to see more.

A few months later I was due to go to my church one evening for a Boys to Men Banquet. This event was held annually in February. On the day of the banquet, I was playing a Batman game on my PlayStation 2. I remember my hormones were jumping for whatever reason. I started reminiscing on the various sex scenes and positions from that one porn flick that I saw. My hormones became uncontrollable; I got antsy and put my video game on pause and began pacing the floor. I sat back down and started grabbing myself, getting myself aroused even more.

It was at that moment I began thinking that for years in school I remembered boys would talk about masturbation or what they called, "beating their meat" and how it felt. So, at this moment I became curious about masturbation, how it felt, what would happen if I tried it. That day I tried it for the first time. At that age and at that time, I recollected hearing the word sperm and that it was a white fluid that came out of a man's penis when he had an orgasm. I never saw it or experienced it, but I wanted to try it. My curiosity built my courage up to give it a try that day. I put my game controller down and got in the shower because I had to get myself together for church, anyway. After I had got out of the shower, I retreated back to my room and sat in that same chair in which I saw my first flick.

I started touching myself yet again. Now mind you, I am butter bald naked, and my curiosity for masturbation is getting deeper by the second. So, I tried it, I began to masturbate. It felt good, and it was getting good. In the middle of my first session at 13 years old, I said to myself, "*Ok it feels good, but where is that white stuff called sperm that makes you feel good when it comes out?*" I was masturbating, but it seemed like it was taking a long time for something "amazing" to happen, so I needed help to get on with the session and make it feel real. I learned quickly that in order to do this I needed something to aid me or this would be a long drawn out first time process. I was also facing the risk of my mom walking in on me, and that would not be good at all having to explain to her what I was doing laid back with my genitals in my hand stroking myself.

I did not have access to that flick my mom's boyfriend showed me months prior. But I needed something to see or visualize to help me reach this orgasm or whatever it was my 13-year-old mind thought I needed to feel. So, I had to conjure up my imagination. I began to imagine myself having sex with a fine full-figured woman. I began thinking about one of my aunt's best friends who I always found attractive even as a little kid. You may laugh, but my preference is older women. My ex-wife was eight years my senior so what does that tell you? But that is how it started for me. It was all a matter of thought. I had my imagination, mental lust dwelling on the thought of me getting intimate with my aunt's best friend at the time.

Once I had the mental image, the feeling I was having during masturbation was beginning to feel real as if what I was imagining was actually happening. I was in a trance, a 4- dimensional state. I felt like a man and that all I needed was one chance to get busy with a real woman and I would rock her world. Ten minutes later I felt something building up down there, and I stopped immediately because it was scaring me. Yet, it was getting good, so I picked back up after 30 seconds of pausing. Before I knew it, I had my first orgasm, and I ejaculated. I remember panting, breathing heavy, and saying to myself, "*What the hell was I waiting for!? This feeling was the best.*" Now I found out what the hype was all about in school.

At that moment, I was hooked! There was no turning back. Like Adam and Eve in the garden, through an experience, I realized I was "naked." Somebody was holding out information on something that brought me joy. It felt like I came to the realization that it was some information about sex and lust that God was holding out on, and He was trying to be mean and only have me find it through marriage which was years down the line if it would happen at all. In actuality, God was in His own way probably trying to tell me to stay away from the tree of knowledge of good and evil so I could find out about sex through marriage, the way He designed it. But like Eve, I was too vulnerable, and like Adam, I was not mature in the spirit to have discernment and awareness that the spirits of lust, perversion, and masturbation were coming to overwhelm me. They all were disguising themselves in the excuses called, "*He's a boy, it's natural;*" "*he's going through puberty;*" "*he's growing up.*" These excuses made me feel comfortable, making way for the addiction to become powerful enough to keep me bound. For years, I welcomed those spirits into my life through the dirt road of vulnerability and curiosity. That first experience altered my life for what I thought would be forever. Before I knew it, I was addicted and loving it. I could not wait until after church that night to have another session. After I had finished that initial session, I cleaned myself up to get rid of the semen. Then, I got dressed and made my way to church.

Chapter 4

Buying into an Addiction

I like to compare a porn addiction to that of a firewall protection software for a computer that you have to buy into before it is considered an addiction. For example, you just bought a laptop. When you open it, you hook it up and start exploring it. A lot of times it comes with a firewall or different type of software available for you to protect your laptop from viruses for 60-90 days as a trial. The reason for the trial is for you to test the product for free and to see if you like it. Once the 60-90-day trial period is up, if you like the software you have to purchase it to continue using it and keeping your computer protected. If you do not buy the software after the trial period, the product stops working and will no longer protect your laptop. If you buy the firewall after the trial period then you have to renew your product subscription every year. If you chose to renew it, sometimes there will be renewal fee. Once you renew the product subscription, the firewall will continue to protect your laptop until your next year of renewal.

Well, that is how a porn addiction is. Once you try it, whether it be looking at pornographic material or masturbation, if you like the pleasure and what it does for you, you then "buy into it." By buying into it, it becomes a habit. That habit turns into an addiction. Before you know it time has gone by, and you look up, and you have been entertaining the addiction for a year. That is until you get a warning message from the Holy Spirit telling you if you keep indulging in this addiction you will lose yourself in it. Sometimes, that message gets overshadowed by the reminiscing of gratification it gave you. If you think like the computer user and you choose to continue to buy back into it after your warning, then you will continue to indulge in the addiction or relapse if you have stopped for a significant time frame.

Although pornography was thrust into my face by my mother's boyfriend, I chose to "buy into it" after that flick was given to me because I liked what I saw. I was not told of the effects the decision would have on my life. Granted I was involved heavily in the church; however, I was also a vulnerable kid. I really did not know the spiritual severity that came with the addiction. Every time I relapsed back into my addiction, it was symbolic that I was "buying back into it." I was a satisfied customer of the devil's software of sin.

When I realized that I was addicted to pornography, and that I was no longer just trying, I was so deep into the addiction that I lost myself and it was hard to get out of it. As a porn addict, like any other addict; e.g., addicted to drugs or alcohol, my objective was to always get that initial feeling, that rush, that high I felt when I first masturbated. I realized that out of the 10 plus years that I was addicted, none of my orgasms during my masturbation sessions matched that first time high I had when I first tried it. For if it did or if any time after the initial try were better than the first, it would have satisfied me enough to stop. After that first time I masturbated, consistent sessions were a norm for me. When I started out the addiction was so bad that I was masturbating three to six time a day, minimum daily. The funny thing was that in my teenage mind I thought that because I did it so much, I would run out of sperm and start shooting dust or something terrible would happen. However, I would not stop until something crazy would happen.

Because of my three to six-times-a-day sessions, my penis would hurt when I would ejaculate or even use the restroom at various times. There would be this numbness I would get in my testicles, I never went to the doctor out of shame. The pain scared me in the beginning because I thought God was punishing me. In turn, I stopped masturbating for a brief period, but it was not long before I was back at it.

It did not take long until I began feeling like an addict. I started to feel as if I could not live without masturbating. In the beginning, I would only masturbate in the privacy of my bedroom as a teenager before school when I got dressed to leave out or after school when I got home. It was not until I got older that anytime I got the urge I could not wait until I got home. I had to take care of business right then and there. It got to a point where I did not care or have regard for where I was. If I was in school as a teenager or when I became an adult and if I was at work, I would retreat to the restroom, lock myself in a stall, and have my session. If I was out shopping and the urge came upon me, I dropped what I was doing or what I had in my hand to find the nearest restroom and gratify myself. I was addicted, and at that point, I realized I was. Keep in mind I was doing this without a cell phone, access to a DVD, or pornographic website. All I had to aid me were the mental images and my imagination.

When I was 13 years old, my mother bought a desktop computer and internet dial-up service. I learned quickly how to surf the internet. After a while, the mental images were no longer enough for me to aid my masturbation sessions and I needed more. I began to feel the need to watch porn to make my masturbation sessions seem more realistic and intimate. Once I was comfortable surfing the web I started searching pornography. Back then we had dial-up internet. Therefore, videos took an extremely long time to load up. So initially I opted to settle for searching for pornographic images. I remember times at home where I would print out various images and pretend I had to use the bathroom just to get the privacy. Yet, the entire time I was in there having a session. Next thing I knew the pictures were not working anymore. I needed to see videos. Like an addict desperate for a fix, I began to not care about getting caught, or the long period it took to download the videos. I did what I had to do to feed the addiction.

I am not sure if my mother realized it, but I spent 95 percent of my time at home in the computer room. I longed for moments when my mother went to work, and her boyfriend was not home, and I had the house to myself because I knew if she was not home I did not have to worry about getting caught. My addiction was so bad that up until the time I met my wife at the time and moved out of my mother's home, I kept a list under my bed of my favorite websites and links to videos I loved. I kept a list because I browsed the web for pornographic websites so much that I would forget which websites had my favorite videos.

During my periods of trying to stop, I always got rid of my lists. Therefore, when I relapsed I always had to regenerate new lists. I used to always hope that my mother would never search my room and find my lists. There was always that chance where she could have changed my bed sheets or been in my room and shifted my mattress the wrong way and found them. I was always paranoid that one day she or someone else would find out and I would become the scum of the earth.

Then it happened. One day my mother found out I was looking at porn and boy was that one of the worse days of my life. It was a Thursday, and I will always remember it because I had "Grow Group" that night, which was Bible study for teens at my church. At that time, my mother was transitioning between jobs, and she was using the computer that night to do some job hunting. I was sitting in my room which was right next door to the computer room. She called my first name with a stern loud tone that made me nervous. I just knew I was in trouble. Any other time when my mother calls me she refers to me by "Dee." But when she is mad like any typical African American parent when their child has done something wrong, they will scream for the child's atten tion by yelling their entire name. It was at that moment when she called my name that I already knew inside that she had found out I was looking at pornography on the internet. After she had called me, I got up and went to the computer room where she was to see what she wanted.

As I approached the door of the computer room, she was pointing to the computer screen saying, "What is this?" On the screen was a search engine page where you could see she was about to type in words in the search engine. Apparently, as she was typing various letters, the history popped up of various recent searches, and she was able to see all the pornographic terms I had been searching such as oral sex, Asian sex, doggy style. I did not know how to erase my search history or URL history, so any keywords I implemented in the search engine were still being saved.

Stuck in shock I, of course, denied it initially when she interrogated me with the same repetitive question of was I looking at pornography on the computer. However, my mother knew I was lying. Parents who raise their kids and spend time with them can tell when they are truthful and when they are lying. She asked me over and over again if I had been searching porn sites. Then it happened. I broke down crying, and I remember saying, "Ma I been trying to stop." She replied, "Stop what?" I wanted to say stop masturbating, but I did not know how to say it. I was scared about what she would do, say or think. I knew she would not understand and there was no point of trying to get her to understand. She asked me one question that to this day I wish I had been honest with her and told her the truth because maybe she would have been able to help me and I would have been saved from an overwhelming addiction to pornography and masturbation.

She asked me if her boyfriend at the time showed me any pornography or if he encouraged me to look at porn. I hesitated with a long pause. It was at that moment that immediately my mind went back to when her boyfriend showed me my first flick. However, because he and I were close, I did not want to get him in trouble with her. So I lied and told her no. That one lie cost me ten plus years of being wrapped up, tangled up, and tied up in an addiction to pornography. May I suggest to any reader, no friendship, relationship, or good standing with any individual(s) is worth your freedom, liberty, and being free from sin and right standing with God. It did not dawn on me that maybe pornography was a problem in their relationship and by her son all of a sudden becoming addicted, she knew automatically where my problem came from. For her, if he was the cause as to why her child was now struggling with pornography maybe she would have been able to help me. I believe the day my mother found out, I was too deep into it to just come out on my own. I was too addicted. I was surprised that my mother did not punch me in the chest or really give me one of her lectures. She did tell me to stay off the computer for a while.

Another factor that kept me indulging further into my addiction was that night I proceeded to go to church for Bible Study. I was very upset because my mom found out, I was confused, and I was really wearing my emotions on my sleeve that night. The scary thing was she did not flip out as I expected her to. I thought she would get me when I least expected her too. But honestly, I think she never brought it back up because she did not know what to do or how to help me. Maybe she did not know that my problem was incredibly bad.

When I arrived at church that night, I needed to talk to somebody. I needed understanding, clarity, guidance, information on what the heck was going on with me. I pulled one of the male adults aside to seek counsel. He was the leader of the "Grow Group" teen Bible study. I told him what happened a few hours earlier at my house with my mother and his response was very nonchalant. He was giving me every reason to believe it was okay. I was not going to hell. He gave me no spiritual consequences, no biblical proof for his rationale at all. I was not spiritually convicted through the conversation nor was I led to a place of repentance. His exact words were, "You're a boy, you are going to look at girls. If it was my son, I'd be glad to find out that you were looking at porn and it was women and not gay porn." My high level of respect for him at the time along with his influence convinced me that I was okay and that my problem was not as bad as I was making it out to be.

That is why I am a firm believer that we have to pay attention to our kids. Find out what their interests are, who they are talking to, and what type of people or things easily influence them. If you can build trust and a strong, healthy relationship with your kids where it is understood on both ends that you have their best interest at heart, that makes it easier for you, as parents, to connect with and minister to them. Instill the Word of God in their lives; pray with them; teach them the necessity in pleasing and living for God, and show them what it means to be the epitome of a young person living for God. When you implement these few steps, you will more likely have a better chance of being a stronger influence on your child's life than anyone else they will interact with in their life.

For me, I was influenced by the gentleman in my church who was clearly not the most saved of all the rest of the male figures there. Within two weeks after my consulting him I was back looking at pornography. My mother did not discuss the spiritual effects nor did she discuss with me how the spirits of lust and perversion would draw me further away from God. She left the issue alone altogether. She probably was not aware that my interest in pornography had grown from curiosity to a full-blown addiction.

The reason was probably that I became very creative and clever in finding ways to feed my addiction without getting caught again. Today, I wish I had a good male spiritual confidant. I could not go to my mother's boyfriend because he was the one who introduced me to pornography; and clearly, he would not give me sound spiritual advice. I could not go to my pastor because I was not comfortable talking to him about this specific issue; plus, I was too embarrassed to go to him. I could not go to my biological father because our relationship was not close enough where I felt comfortable enough to go to him. Lastly, the only real male figure I had was my maternal grandfather. I could not go to him either because he was not saved nor in church and he would have given me the same advice as any average male. My issue with my grandfather was deeper than him not being saved. A few years prior I witnessed a few events between him and my grandmother and I found out about his infidelity. Therefore, I did not trust him nor anything he had to say about steering me in the right direction as far as manhood was concerned.

As I had gotten older into my teen years, of course, puberty and the raging of my hormones were in full effect. For me, I believe there was a bigger factor that kept me bound in my addiction. Growing up, I felt ugly and fat and I had self-esteem and rejection issues when it came to girls. I was never the popular kid in school nor did I have many girlfriends. Not only that, but I was shy, and I did not know how to approach a girl I was attracted to or wanted to date. If I did build up the nerve to approach them, they did not take me seriously, or I was just thrown in the friend zone. It seemed like I was never good enough to be taken serious in romantic relationships. When it came to females, I always got hurt or taken advantage of, or she just would not love me for me. I wanted to feel loved. I wanted a woman to stare me in the eyes and tell me how much she loved me. I wanted her to touch me a certain kind of way, moan and groan, and make me feel needed and wanted—to feel like a man was supposed to feel.

To keep me from sinking into a deep depression, I turned to masturbation and pornography to help me cope with all that festered up pain and rejection I was feeling. I remember when I was in high school the girls were very well built and developed with breasts and bottoms. I conjured up quite a few of them mentally in my masturbation sessions. I imagined myself having intercourse with the girls from my school while masturbating. This was life all throughout high school; my addiction was a big secret. My interest, curiosity, and trying to cope with pain were nothing but ingredients that created a cancerous addiction that was killing me spiritually and naturally.

Chapter 5

Art Gallery of the Mind

With the sexual arousal, excitement, and sometimes pleasure that pornographic material can bring to a person, we do not stop to think how powerful pornography is in a cognitive sense. With the eyes being a gateway to the mind, most of the cherished events in our lives, what we often call memorable moments become memories simply because our eyes bore witness to everyday living. Our eyes capture the precious moments as well as the horrific moments of life. That is why 20 years later we can press the rewind button in our minds and relive the times that made us laugh, cry, and grow.

When you reminisce with family and friends about the past, it is easy to catch yourself saying the cliché, "I remember it like it was yesterday." A lot of times you do remember it very vividly! That is how powerful mental images (memory) are. Mental images or visuals can be ever so clear and make you feel like you are there even though it happened years ago. How the mind records, stores, and replays events from life is incredibly vicious and amazing. It works the same when pornography and sexual images or visuals of people to whom we are attracted slip through our eye gates; it is stored in our mind.

Pornographic images and videos to the mind are like a tattoo on human skin. It is hard to get rid of it unless you have surgery.

But even after the surgery, it will still leave a mark as a reminder that it was once there. Once you watch those enticing videos, it is hard to erase them from your mind unless you go into deep spiritual surgery—prayer, fasting, and consecration—to ask God to relieve your mind of the mental torment and staining that comes with the porn addiction. Request Him to take the taste out of our mouth and change our taste buds for spiritual things.

The mere fact that it is hard to get rid of the visuals of pornographic material in the mind is what makes the images and imagination so powerful. It is in the times when we try to turn away from masturbation and pornography that those images and videos we watched that turned us on and to which we gave our undivided attention can easily be replayed in the mind. That can get us to a place where we relapse on a consistent basis and make deliverance from the addiction a difficult process. It is indeed the power one's mind has of being able to replay vividly pornographic material that the mind itself becomes one of the strongest obstacles in overcoming an addiction and seeking deliverance.

Pornography is an art to the eye in the art gallery of the mind because it is always available to observe for however long you choose to view it. A person who loves art goes to an art gallery and for hours will look at all kinds of paintings and sculptures. They will become fascinated by how the artwork ignites their imagination. The imagination of what the art really means, how it makes them feel, how it accurately expresses how they feel, and how they could find their very essence in the art becomes fascinating.

Many directors and actors in the porn industry view pornography as beautiful artwork. They are passionate as well as proud of the work they generate. Meanwhile, for many porn addicts, the work itself brings them stimulation and a false sense of a strong 4- dimensional sexual experience by way of playing on a person's imagination. Pornographic images have the power to keep your imagination going. The various pornographic images, videos, and imagination along with masturbation help a person get a 4-dimensional experience as if they are having intercourse with those very attractive people that are performing or posing in the videos or still images that are being viewed.

The videos and images are very much misleading. When the various actors perform, often times they look into the camera as if they are looking directly into the eyes of every viewer making the viewer think and feel as if they are wanted and needed; and during masturbation as if they are being satisfied by the viewer themselves. For the viewer, every groan, moan and scream the actors make on camera makes them feel as if it is geared towards them or it is happening as a result of them. This kind of power plays on the minds of porn addicts and is powerful in keeping them bound to the addiction itself. Addicts who wrestle with self-esteem issues, and are often told they are unattractive, and have a hard time finding companionship tend to turn to pornography for solace. They also tend to stay in the never-ending cycle of the addiction because porn has given them a watered down counterfeit form of intimacy. They are not being told they are unattractive, or they do not feel as if they are worthless and unwanted sexually.

As a former addict, I had favorite videos and images that I used as material to aid my masturbation sessions and bring my fantasies to life. As I mentioned earlier, I knew the URL addresses and how to find my favorite materials on the internet. I had URL addresses handwritten on a list I kept hidden in between my mattress or in a secret place no one would be likely to find. To this day those once-upon-a-time favorite images and videos of women in various erotic positions are still vivid and clear in my mind. No matter how much I try, I cannot get rid of the visuals, the images, and videos that are stored in my mind, at least not by my own power or might. These mental images that are still ever so fresh in my mind had once upon a time been so powerful that they hindered me from deliverance and sobriety of the addiction.

There were times when I would go days, weeks, or sometimes months without watching pornography and masturbating. During those temporary moments of sobriety, I remember I used to feel like I was on top of the world and that once and for all I had conquered my addiction. Then all of a sudden, throughout a particular day during my sobriety period those same images and videos would pop up in my head. Immediately, my hormones would skyrocket and get to raging. I would get weak and vulnerable to the clear, vivid images I used to watch that were forever trapped in my mind. Before I knew it, I had relapsed back into watching pornography and masturbating. Then the feeling of defeat and the feeling as if I was a low down dirty hypocrite came upon me. The feeling of condemnation began to suffocate my salvation and become a pot hole in my walk with God. I was secretly ashamed because it was true, my actions were showing that I loved my sinful addiction more than God.

In between my relapsing phases, it was always the same cycle. Those powerful images and videos would come from out of nowhere in my mind. For example, I could be thinking about something productive then suddenly my mind would go from productive thinking to an image of my favorite porn star bent over, jiggling her backside in one of my favorite videos. It would scare me because it always happened randomly.

When it would happen, I would go into mild panic attacks. I would experience heavy breathing. In a sense, it felt like my conscious and spiritual convictions sent me into panic mode because it is at that moment that I am aware something in my cognitive triggered my addiction and now my flesh is weak, and I feel myself giving into gratifying my flesh. It was also during those moments where it felt like I was constantly in the biggest fight of my life because I was wrestling with the thought that I did not want to upset God to the point that my sins were the reasons He takes me up out of here. For me, during those times it was a tug-of-war with God and my flesh. I recall quite often before relapsing I would spend a good five to ten minutes weighing the pros and cons in my decision as to whether I should relapse or not. I remember saying to myself quite often, "Dee don't give in; you were doing good; you went a long period; you can live without this." "Dee, you are a hypocrite, you'll be just like the rest of the hypocrites and perverted preachers; it'll be a matter of time before God exposes you if you don't stop now." Meanwhile, I was simultaneously convincing myself that it was okay to relapse.

You must always be careful what you watch because what you watch can and will scar you for life. It is the same as when a kid or even an adult who witnesses a tragic event. It can affect that individual for years because that kid or that adult cannot get out of their head the mental image of the moment they saw someone gunned down and the scenery that followed. War veterans today suffer from Post-Traumatic Stress Disorder (PTSD) because of traumatic events during a war that they experienced firsthand. Veterans suffer because of the mental images they saw that are still fresh in their mind even five to ten years later. Even years after their tenure of participating in war, they experience the panic attacks, cold sweats at night because the mental images haunt them. I experienced the same struggles with my addiction to pornography. The only difference is that when it comes to pornography, you have the power to either choose to watch it and allow the things you witness to stain your mind or not. If I can help someone who may be curious about pornography, please do not entertain it because the spirit of perversion that manhandles the enticing appeal of pornography is overwhelming and you will be enrolling yourself for a spiritual fight with a lust demon that you may not be prepared to fight.

Because of the fact that I was aware of the intense amount of power that lies within the pornographic material, my ex-wife and I were very cautious with our children in terms of what they watched, entertained, and engaged in on television and social media. My two step-sons were becoming teenagers at the time, as well, so we had to deal with the reality that they were beginning to have an interest in females and that they would be experiencing changes in their hormones. They were beginning to know what it meant to be horny. Therefore, we had to educate and prepare them rather than let television educate them. Hollywood gets more perverted as the days go by. From the commercials to the talk shows and even G-rated movies, all will have sexual references in them that you will only catch if you pay close attention. So much perverted content is available to our children, but we do not pay attention to it because of the misconception that cartoons in the 21st century are clean and free of sexual gestures and references. Many explicit messages can come across our children's eyes in a matter of seconds, and those messages can come on so strong and powerful as it pertains to sexual content that as parents we must be cautious.

From experience, as a child, all it took was a few seconds for a seed to be planted. As time goes on and the individuals who generate the various television shows become more creative and clever about how they implement and expose sexual content to our children, I can imagine the sexual content our children will have come across their innocent faces at such young ages. One of my greatest fears is worrying that one day my sons will fall to this same curse because of the uncertainty of their ability to be able to overcome the powerful, addictive, overwhelming spirit of lust and perversion that manhandles pornography. As a parent, my duty is to preserve my kids' purity and protect them from things that can contaminate their mind and strip them of their innocence.

For men in general, when it comes to our love and admiration for women, we thrive off or get excitement from the visuals we can mentally conjure up of very attractive women that could be doing nothing more than merely standing in our presence. For example, a man could be at the supermarket. While he is in aisle nine, there is a very attractive woman looking at the canned vegetables, not paying him any attention. She has all the curves and right skin tone, and he cannot help but stare. While staring, the man will mentally undress her with his eyes and say things to himself like, "If I had one night with her" or "Man, I'd like to see what's underneath them jeans."

It is the visual, that potent sexual image, we can create and replay in our minds that get us going. A man will look at a woman and imagine himself having sex with her. The imagination will feel so clear and be quite vivid. The very thought of the sexual intercourse puts the key in the ignition to his hormones, and it has the potential to make him feel like he has to go to the restroom or in a private place to please himself through masturbation. Just because you had a sexual moment in your mind does not mean you have to go forth and gratify your flesh. Get a hold of the mental images before they get a hold of you.

Chapter 6

Bringing a Porn Addiction
To Your Marriage

Every now and again, you will hear a testimony, read an article, or come across an individual through conversation who was or is currently a porn addict; they may be single or even dating someone. Not too often is it common to read about a married person battling a porn addiction. I am not ashamed to say that I am one of those rare people who have that testimony. I was addicted to porn and feeding my addiction when I met, dated, and married my ex-wife. I made the hideous decision to bring my porn addiction into my marriage. I was not made aware that porn addictions had the power to ruin marriages. I had one problem already, and that was battling an addiction to pornography by my individual self, but I created an additional dilemma when I let my addiction run rampant for so long under my ex-wife's nose during our marriage.

The truth was in the beginning when I started dating my ex-wife, even in the infancy of our relationship, I was frightened— frightened to tell her about my addiction and that at that time it was at the point that things had gotten out of hand. My need for self-gratification was outrageous. I do not believe my ex-wife, in the beginning, understood how deep my addiction was. Quite frankly, I do not recall her even knowing I had a porn addiction back then because I was what you call a functional addict. I am a private person by nature; therefore, I kept my addiction very private even from my ex-wife.

By the time I met her I was too far gone into my addiction. However, I never showed evidence that I had a problem. I did not talk about pornography or give her a clue that I was even interested in pornography. The only way one would have known that I had a pornography addiction was if they caught me masturbating or looking at porn, found my secret porn list or I trusted them so much that I shared the truth about my addiction with them. Functional addicts will feed their addiction and maneuver in life as if nothing is wrong. However, behind closed doors, it is open season for indulgence.

I was scared to tell my ex-wife or even have an in-depth conversation with her about it. There was the fear that I was never sure how she would respond to me if I was honest with her. Would she judge me? Would she want to divorce? Would she be able to handle me and help me seek deliverance? Would she lose respect for me and look at me differently? These were the questions and concerns I had. I always had an inclination that some way or somehow my secret struggle would be exposed to the world and I was going to need her support. There I was, in too deep into my addiction and the one person with whom I was supposed to be able to share anything, I felt like it was impossible to even be transparent with her about my addiction.

The night before my wedding I went through changes. My ex-wife and I were shacking up until the day we married. We agreed that the night before our wedding we would follow the tradition of not seeing each other and the next time we would meet would be at the altar. She spent the night at one of her girlfriend's house. Meanwhile, I stayed home with the boys. That night I remember trying to clean my slate with God because I did not want to bring my addiction into my marriage. I was repenting and asking God to forgive me for all the fornicating my ex-wife and I had done, for all the pornography I had watched, and the masturbation in which I indulged.

I was about to become a married man within a couple of hours, and I wanted my wife at the time, to be the only one I desired to see in the nude and lust after. Yet, even in my repentance that night, the urge to watch pornography was building up at a rapid pace. I was panicking because I begin to realize that the addiction was still in my system and it was not trying to make an exit any time soon. My repentance turned into me begging God to deliver me that night. Somehow, I convinced myself that the only way to get it all out of my system was to watch pornography and masturbate one last time. I did not have a bachelor party, but for me that was it.

I went into my secret stash and retrieved my porn DVD that my little cousin had given me some years prior. I made sure the boys were sound asleep so that when I got going, I would not have any interruptions. Once they were asleep, I popped the DVD in my PlayStation 2 and had a field day. But boy was I naïve in thinking that it was all out of my system that night.

The truth is, I watched pornography and surfed for pornographic sites while I was married. Of course, I had to be cautious and sneaky about my addiction because I did not want my wife to find out or for her to blow up over it. I was not a single man anymore. After a while, I begin to notice that my addiction began to slowly affect the sexual intercourse I was having with my ex-wife.

When a person watches pornography and masturbates, they do not want to experience the embarrassment of being caught in the act by your parent, child, spouse, etc. This was the case for me. Therefore, it was always a need to rush and hurry up to reach my orgasm. Not only did I not want to get caught, but I was simply rushing my session to hurry up and reach my orgasm so that I could feel that high I felt when I first tried it. As a teenager, I remember rushing my masturbation sessions and striving to ejaculate quickly so my mom would never walk in on me. The problem came when I brought that mentality and same eagerness into my sex life with my ex-wife in the marriage bed.

During intercourse with my ex-wife if she would have gone slowly it would not have mattered. Her strokes would easily send me into orgasm mode vastly. For me, it was the excitement along with being anxious. On top of that all of those mental images, imaginations, and porn materials I used to generate in my 4-dimensional masturbation sessions were feeling real. My fantasies were like dreams coming true.

Yet, my intercourse somehow was not enough to keep me away from the hardcore porn and soft porn. There were times during my marriage when I would wake up in the morning, grab my phone, and go into the bathroom and lock the door. I would get on YouTube and type in keywords to pull up twerk videos.

Or if I was really horny, I would browse the web on my phone for pornographic sites and masturbate. All the while, my ex-wife was still in bed sleeping. I also had moments where I could not wait for her and the kids to go out and leave me in the house by myself because I would have a field day. My sessions were stress relievers. I went through so much in my marriage at the time, and porn helped me escape temporarily and cope with the issues, or at least I thought.

There was a season where I had masturbated and looked at pornography so much during my marriage that it was sometimes hard to have sex with my wife. I did not have the energy or the desire to do so because in those cases I had already satisfied myself sexually in a session somewhere in a bathroom unbeknown to her. However, the reality was that I had an addiction that took control of me because I failed to get a handle on it.

My problem was I had not one to talk to, no one I could confide in and be my raw self about my struggle so that they could help me before I got to a posture where I was dragging an addiction as such into my marriage. For years, I wanted to go to some type of rehabilitation center, but then I figured people would question my whereabouts and interrogate me and I did not want that. I was known to be a young preacher, quiet and into God, a good boy. Therefore, I did not want to ruin people's good views of me and risk trashing my character because the world knows a flaw about me.

As much as I was in church, there were no spiritual mentors I trusted or that I could get a hold of with whom I felt comfortable reaching out. I felt stuck and by myself. I used to always think that I would have to take this secret to my grave and pray to God that when I stood before Him, I would be truthful about my sin. However, I prayed that hopefully He at least would charge me with this sinful crime as a misdemeanor and let me in the gates of heaven. A soul with no spiritual guidance and no one to hold it accountable is headed for destruction.

My desire for help and the chance to come clean and be heard became a reality between March and April of 2015. During that time, my ex-wife and I had gone through a serious falling out. After we lashed out very badly towards each other, we eventually apologized. I began to notice that we fell out too often, and we had to get to the bottom of why it happened so much and so often. We went down the list to figure out what type of baggage or broken-ness we brought into the marriage that was causing constant rifts between us.

One night we took a drive to grab dinner and for the first time we were honest, upfront, and detailed about the dirt and strug-gles we brought into our marriage. For the first time, I was able to come clean to her about my addiction to pornography, and I went on to tell her that I was guilty of looking at pornography and masturbating while being married to her. Her response amazed me. She was understanding and told me I could overcome the ad-diction. She went on to speak highly of me. Most importantly I felt relieved that I was no longer living a lie and keeping a secret. It was the first step in terms of me exposing myself and a giant step to seeking my deliverance.

Prior to this particular event, my ex-wife and I would watch pornography together, and we would be intimate while watching it. I was always hesitant because I knew what porn did to me, how it made me feel, and the overall struggle I was having with it. A lot of times we watched it together when I had been clean for a long period. Then watching it with her triggered my addiction, and before I knew it, I was back sneaking a look at it and having masturbation sessions behind her back.

As for her, I assume she may have thought bringing pornography into the marriage would spice up the intimacy in the bedroom. She wanted me to watch pornography to learn new positions and techniques. However, she did not understand the severity of what watching pornography did to me. It caused me to be more into the female actors than her. Part of the reason why I continued to entertain my addiction was to cope with other problems I was facing internally between my wife and me that were crushing my self-esteem. I always felt as if my ex-wife was comparing me to her former partners. Rather than her creating new memories with me and just experimenting with each other's bodies, she wanted me to touch her like the last man did. It was frustrating, and because of that I always watched pornography during our marriage because I did not get complaints and comparisons from the female actors who stared back into the camera at me while moaning and groaning as I touched myself. From experience, I conclude that watching pornography as a couple is a huge no-no; especially, if you know your spouse has an addiction to pornography. The truth of the matter is yes, you may be watching the flick together; yes, you may even feel more comfortable with the mere fact that you are watching it with your spouse rather than sneaking around behind their back; however, the effects porn has on the individual will still be there.

In life, there may be moments where we will find others more attractive than our spouses. Most times the actors in pornographic films will be more attractive than our spouses. That partly explains why folks who are married are more into the actors and find themselves greatly desiring pornography and often are more sexually gratified through pornography and masturbation than through intimacy with their spouses. Just think about it, the goal of all creators behind the numerous pornographic movies is to hire actors with the best sex appeal, shape, pretty face, and so on. When you watch these extremely attractive porn stars have sex in every position known to man, it puts those images in the addict's head. Rather than imagining yourself fulfilling those intimate positions with your spouse, you will find yourself imagining being intimate with the porn stars themselves or people you may know who resemble them. This can plant seeds and create a brand-new issue of possible adultery in the near future because now you are curious about what sex would be like with a person you may know, all because of a thought.

I remember one time in particular when my ex-wife and I were being intimate, we decided to watch pornography. We tried every position the porn stars did; I was having the time of my life, or so I thought. One of my favorite porn stars, who went by the name "Cherokee," was on the screen. While I was intimate with my then wife, I found my eyes continuously glued to the television screen. What was happening was that while I was intimate physically with my ex-wife, my mind was imaging that it was "Cherokee." While

I was "feeling" my ex-wife during intimacy, I wanted "Cherokee" and imagined it being her. I felt so dirty and guilty afterward because I was intimate with a porn star that I had never met and who did not even know I exist.

The truth is even in that I was lusting after another woman. It is one thing to lust after another person other than your spouse, but it is something else when you get intimate with your spouse and give them your all times ten during intercourse, making passionate love to them not because they turn you on so much, but because you had someone else on your mind during that intimate moment. Having to conjure up another person mentally during intimate moments with your spouse is dangerous territory.

Prayerfully, I can help someone who happens to find themselves in this situation. If you are about to get married and have an addiction to pornography, please, do not bring your porn addiction into your marriage. Before you get married, be fair with your potential spouse and let them know about your struggle. Give them a chance to decide if they want to fight your demon(s) with you. Too many times we have things we struggle with secretly prior to coming into a covenant through marriage. Then when we tie the knot and all of a sudden, our secret struggles start coming out and our spouses get upset with us, getting frustrated to the point where they no longer want to be bothered with us, we get confused. Confused to the point where we throw in their face the vows that were made, "For better or for worse." However, the truth is initially you never exposed the worse of you to the point where they could make a decision to choose if they wanted to take on your struggles for a lifetime. Instead, you gave them a watered down false image of yourself.

Chapter 7

Saved and Addicted to Porn

Is it possible to be saved, sanctified, Holy Ghost filled, fired baptized, and addicted to porn? YES! If that is the case then we have to ask other questions: How prevalent are the issues of pornography or sex in general in the church? Why is the issue of sex, promiscuity, and perversion either kept undercover or a mystery? The truth of the matter is the subject of pornography or sexual perversion in general, is taboo in the church. No one wants to talk about the realities of the saints struggling with the demon of lust. No one wants to talk about the truths in what I call the "church streets." No one wants to discuss why musicians have countless children all over the cities where they serve as minister of music. No one wants to talk about the preacher who uses his power, status, pedigree, and influence to manipulate the panties off of countless women. No one wants to talk about the secret homosexual choir director who struggles with his sexuality because he was molested at a young age. All of these scenarios have a root. Pornography and other sexual perversions have plagued marriages and triggered behaviors that eventually have the potential to bring harm to other people emotionally, mentally, and spiritually.

There are barely any churches, ministries, or what have you that can dedicate their time, money, and resources to help porn addicts or at least take the time to address the addiction itself or provide information. The reason is probably that the church has failed to find an approach to deal with the issue. I believe with any issue that comes up when you do not know how to address it you will not touch it. There are researchers, doctors, and the like who spend years trying to find cures for various sicknesses and cancers; they have possible solutions, but they do not have all the answers. That does not stop them from asking for the help, resources, and funds to do the research to find various cures and solutions. It should be the same way with a porn addiction. No one may have all the answers, but we have to start somewhere; at least address what we do know.

When it comes to the church's view of pornography, specifically Protestant, charismatic churches, they have a broad generic view on the subject of sex. It is never anything specific. Various church leaders may be opinionated about the subject and may verbally express personal opinions, but as a church, in general, there is no clear stance on pornography, how to address it or how to offer help and deliverance for addicts. Whether it be pornography, masturbation, or lust, it all tends to fall under the general topic of "sex" when the church talks about it. Often times there is no breakdown in sermons, no clear understanding of the various classifications and levels of sex and perversion. However, it is clear that the church, in general, is against sex outside of marriage. That much we do know.

However, the truth of the matter is pornography has always been very prevalent in the church. It is so prevalent that the Apostle Paul wrote letters to the Corinthian church addressing the sexual immorality that was taking place. He addressed spiritual leaders in terms of how they should handle the issue and how the saints should conduct themselves.

In the Old Testament, 2 Samuel, chapter 11, we find the story of David and Bathsheba. In this particular story, we discover that David has two problems. One, he has a lust problem. He cannot help but sexually admire and visually see himself sexually with Bathsheba. Two, he has a coveting problem. Because of his failure to control his sexual desire for her, he has to have her. However, it is not the issue of having her; the real issue is she was Uriah's wife at the time. I stated earlier in the previous chapter that pornography, even sex or lust in general, has the potential to bring harm to other people. With that in mind, as we continue to read the story of David and Bathsheba, we find that David has sexual relations with Bathsheba. He learns that Bathsheba is pregnant with his child. It is impossible to conclude that her husband Uriah is the father of the child, for Scripture stated that he had been away fighting the Ammonites. David comes up with an idea of sending for Uriah with the façade of giving him rest. While Uriah is home from battle, David encourages Uriah to get intimate with his wife so it would make sense that he was, in fact, the father because she conceived around the time of his intermission from the battle.

Because of Uriah's loyalty, he was too concerned about the battle to even want to be intimate with his wife. When David sees that his plan to cover up his sin failed he sends Uriah back to battle with instructions to put him on the front line to have him killed. Once Uriah was killed, David was able to immediately take Bathsheba as his wife and make it seem as if she conceived soon after they married and his sin would therefore not be exposed before the nation. The problem was, Uriah had to lose his life over something that rightfully belonged to him, all because David did not have a handle on his lust problem and his desire to have

Bathsheba. Not only did Uriah lose his life, but the baby that was the by-product of David and Bathsheba's affair ended up dying as a result of David's sin.

David then had another child, Solomon. I would suggest that Solomon's addiction to women was greater than his father, David. Scripture records that Solomon had 700 wives and 300 concubines. What is the need for a man to have 700 wives and 300 concubines? Unless we were to suggest that Solomon had a lust problem, an addiction to women that not just one woman could satisfy him. This is a perfect example of a generational curse passed down from parent to child. Not only was the generational curse passed down but it became stronger and more perverted and ridiculously out of control.

If we do not make sound decisions to get delivered from our addictions we put our children at risk of having to eventually wrestle with the same struggles and be greatly overtaken all because they saw mom and dad wrestle with it. If there is no clear evidence of the parent making an effort to bring the addiction under subjection, it sends a message to the child that it is okay to indulge in the behavior and or addiction because they learned it at home. In turn, it makes it hard to even chastise your child. How can a parent chastise their child for doing something they are still partaking in themselves?

Through the instructions of Scripture, we as believers have a duty to flee from sexual immorality. The Apostle Paul wrote in 1 Corinthians 6:18 (NIV), *"Flee from sexual immorality. All other sins a person commits are outside the body, but whoever sins sexually, sins against their own body."* The Apostle Paul suggests in the latter part of the verse that we do our own selves a disservice when we are guilty of sexual immorality. The Apostle Paul goes on to say that our bodies belong to God. Therefore, we do not have the authority to gratify ourselves as we see fit. We as believers do not belong to ourselves. Christ bought us with a price at Calvary. It is indeed our responsibility to honor Him with a holy lifestyle that is free from lust and sexual immorality.

In the Bible, idol worshippers would commit acts of sexual immorality in temples unto their gods. Anything you give too much attention to and or your undivided attention to more than the God of the Biblical Canon becomes your God. It is the same with pornography and those who are addicted to it. When an addict yields to the addiction more than he yields to God, then it becomes his idol and his god, because he has more regard for it than the God he claims to serve. This type of yielding can lead an addict to habitually indulge in all types of acts of sexual immorality.

We live in a time now just like in the time of the Apostle Paul. The church today has a strong spirit of perversion that is running rampant. In churches all over the country, members are sleeping with each other; preachers are sleeping with members. Ministers of music are having babies all over the city in which they reside with women from different congregations. Sometimes they impregnate multiple women at the same time that attend the same church. Various organizations have annual conferences, conventions, or convocations. A lot of times during these events church goers utilize the time and opportunity to have affairs, fornicate, or just simply indulge in sexual sin of all types.

The spirit of perversion is not dealt with in the church in the way that it should be. When it comes to sex, perversion, adultery, pornography or even pregnancy out of wedlock, the church always seems to be reactive rather than preventive or proactive. For example, most times we do not talk about sex before marriage until a young woman gets pregnant and she is not married. The church, for the most part, does not deal with perversion until it comes out that two men in the church were engaged in homosexual activity.

The Apostle Paul dealt with the issues of sexual immorality and perversion head on. In Ephesians 5:3 (NIV) he writes, *"But among you there must not be even a hint of sexual immorality, or of any kind of impurity, or of greed, because these are improper for God's holy people."* Verse five then says, *"For of this you can be sure: No immoral, impure or greedy person — such a person is an idolater — has any inheritance in the Kingdom of Christ and of God."* Here again, we see Paul addressing the sexual immoral as idolaters and that they have no place in God's kingdom. Yet, he starts verse three by saying that there shall be no hint of sexual immorality among the believers. The problem is that believers today flaunt their sins and addictions with no remorse. The reason why saints these days seem to have no remorse is that there is a lack of accountability.

A genuine person who is serious about their walk with Christ will never feel comfortable in their sin even if they wrestle with it in private when no one is watching them. For me, I was always conscious about my addiction. I always felt guilty. However, it is a tug-of-war in mind and spirit. When you have pornographic material in hand, you have your privacy where no one can catch you.

You make the decision if you should or should not masturbate. My flesh would always overwhelm my spirit man to the point where I would submit to my flesh and hurry up to finish my session(s) just to get that feeling I felt when I first tried it. I call it the first "high." Immediately, when I was done, the guilt and shame were incredibly unbearable.

There I was, young, saved, chasing after the things of God, with an addiction I could not shake nor did anyone know that I was wrestling with. I was frightened to go to anyone for help out of fear of being looked at as dirty, impure, and condemned. I always had frequent conversations with God through prayer. Most times, my conversations would always start out with me confessing, "*God, I have a problem. Please do not take me out for my failure to comply with the standard of holiness You set in Your Word.*" I always felt that because I did not steal, smoke, drink, or have physical sex outside of marriage I was fine because those were the most obvious deadly sins in the church. In my mind, I felt as though because I had what I felt was this minor technicality behind closed doors, which was a little lust problem with women through the avenue of pornography, I was not that bad off. But the truth of the matter is that sin is sin, no matter how big or small. What I loved about myself was the fact that no matter how terrible the habit became for me, I was always transparent with God about my struggle.

Because I had no one to confide in about my addiction, for years, it felt as if I was the only young preacher wrestling with a porn addiction. I felt this way because there was no one talking about it; there were no seminars, conferences, rehabilitation centers that I knew of where people like me could find themselves comfortably addressing lust issues and how to overcome it. The idea of going to my pastor at the time was not an option because I feared the reaction of being judged and or possibly my struggle being the sermon topic the following Sunday. I feared being treated differently as if I was a disease. In the end, as God began to bring me out to a place of deliverance from my addiction to pornography, I gradually began to lose the feeling of being ashamed. I began to find out that fellow constituents (pastors) who I had a high regard for had the same struggle as I did and sometimes even worse. I found out they were in the same posture that I was in and that posture was in a place of asking ourselves a series of questions. *How did I get here? How do I get a grasp on my iniquities and regain self-control, discipline?* Most importantly, *who do I go to in order to get the help I need?*

Being saved, a believer of Jesus Christ, and wrestling with lust or an addiction of any kind will draw you away from Christ especially when you know what God requires of you and that He will hold you accountable. Luke 12:48 faithfully declares, *To whom much is given, much is required of you.* God has given so much to us, whether it be sparing us from sickness, car accidents, harm or danger. He requires the simple thing, and that is to live a consecrated life. It is hard to be a believer and feel comfortable in sin and either not feel God's wrath or know that He is upset. Proverbs 3:12 states, *"For the Lord chastises those He loves, as a father the son He delights in."*

For me it was difficult being exposed to pornographic material and becoming addicted at an early age, trying to manage my hormones on top of knowing that I have a gift and a call on my life and trying to operate in my call. One must have a desire to do right and be upstanding before God as much as possible. It is difficult indeed when the desires you have are normal; however, the dilemma is not the desires that you have, but when you convince yourself that it is okay to cater to, entertain, and fulfill the desires of your flesh.

We as believers of Christ have to accept the reality that we all have struggles that we battle with beyond belief. Week after week, we go to church, dance, shout, speak in unknown tongues, pay tithes, give monetary seed offerings, and go home still wrestling, still broken, and looking for answers and way out of the various struggles we face. Some leaders in the body of Christ today do a stupendous disservice to parishioners when they collect their weekly monetary donations, but provide no solutions to the struggles of everyday life. The only advice that is mostly given is when the preachers tell the believers to dance or shout their problems away. That is not enough. It is hideous to realize that out of all financial sacrificing, loyalty, and commitment parishioners contribute to their churches, their internal struggles continuously go unaddressed.

Often parishioners pay no attention to the need to have their internal struggles addressed by the church because, most of the time, the focus, especially for charismatic Protestant churchgoers, is that they had a good time in church and they had a good dance during a praise break. These days we are given a "fix" and not a solution to get rid of "it," whatever the person's "it" is. Part of the reason this happens way too often is that some leadership in churches today are more concerned about acquiring preaching engagements, building a name for themselves, and looking good rather than bringing souls to Christ. Nor do they tend to care about making the focal point of their ministry the condition, well-being, and upkeep of one's soul. It is my firm belief that once we as an entire church make the well-being of souls the focal point in ministry, we can almost guarantee that a slew of folks who are bound by various spirits and addictions will begin to experience true deliverance. It will be at that moment where our preaching and evangelism will no longer be in vain.

Chapter 8

Teenage Porn Addicts

No one is exempt from temptation(s) and or the possibility of being exposed to or becoming victims of an addiction to pornography or other sexual perversions. We must keep in mind that the spirit of lust as well as the spirit of perversion has no age range or age limit. They attack whoever is willing and vulnerable to entertain and render their attention unto them. However, of all the potential victims of pornography, the risk of teenagers (and even preteenagers) being exposed to sexual content and eventually becoming candidates to have an addiction to pornography or engage in other sexually immoral acitivities is at an all-time high.

Teenagers are easy targets because they have access to social media, websites, cable networks, magazines and digital material such as DVDs that provide exposure to pornographic images and scenarios that have all the potential to spark their interest, grab their attention, and get their mind going. Teenagers have sexual conversations among their peers. The peer pressure of having sex at an early age is also real. A teenager's mind functions on the fuel of curiosity. I know this because it was the curiosity I had as a teenager that got me going and addicted to pornography.

When I was married, my eldest stepson was a teenager about 13 years old at the time. He had his bouts with puberty, and he was beginning to start having an interest in girls. His hormones started raging in ways beyond his comprehension, and he needed direction and guidance so he would not make the same mistakes I made by using pornography and masturbation as a way to release and self-gratify himself. His mother and I were foreign to dealing with this issue as parents because he was the first one of our five children to become a teenager where we had to have the conversation with him about sex. Therefore, how we dealt with him on the topic was more like trial and error. It was very critical for us as parents because how we dealt with him would shape how we dealt with our other children as they reached their teen years and began facing the same issues.

We slowly began to talk to him about scenarios and potential realistic encounters he could have with females. As a man, I knew that he was a teenager who would begin to have urges to have sex. It was necessary to ensure he had some type of lesson on discipline and self-control so he would know that he could not touch girls inappropriately, how to conduct himself, and respect whatever girl he decided to date in his life.

I remember when he was about to go to his first school dance. I made sure that he and I had an in-depth conversation prior to him attending the dance. In all honesty, I felt the conversation was necessary and vital because I understood the time we live in, what happens at parties these days, what it does to teenage boys, and how various encounters with females can trigger curiosity about sex in his mind. He and I are only ten years apart from each other in age. Therefore, it was not that long ago since I was a teenager and I went to various parties and danced with females. The times have not changed that much. I know how vulgar things can get.

The idea of him going to the party concerned me because I was not naïve. I knew he was going to dance with females and the way girls dance with boys these days with all the grinding, dry humping, and twerking females do on the male genitals has infinite potential to get his mind going and desire more on a greater scale. With his mind going, it would, therefore, take him mentally to explore sexual fantasies which can then lead to his curiosity and interest in porn; therefore, making him vulnerable to becoming addicted.

What made his situation even worse was that he was technically the son of a preacher. So, the pressure, guilt, and spiritual attack would be even greater because of the household from which he came. It is important to keep in mind the pressure that preacher's kids go through, the pressure of knowing that everyone is not just watching them but their entire family is under a microscope. People are expecting you to act a certain way as if you are not expected to have shortcomings or make mistakes. The pressure can be too much; I am well aware of that because I am a preacher's kid myself.

One would be surprised that preacher's kids, or "PKs" as they are called, can be some of the most jacked up people on the face of the planet because most times there is no one for them to talk to. At times when they do mess up and want to confide in someone, they have to be cautious. They may confide in the wrong person who may not mind sharing their struggles with other people. If that happens, they risk having their iniquities bring shame to their parents and their work in ministry, ultimately making them look bad. Not only that, but who wants to be under public scrutiny?

You will find a lot of "PKs" are drug abusers, alcoholics, porn addicts, sex addicts, depressed, and wrestling with stuff beyond imagination. The biggest misconception is with all the spiritual power and anointing their parents may have, "PKs" are less likely to struggle with issues of the flesh.

It is vital that we take the time to educate our children on the necessity of self-control when it comes to sex and their hormones. Uncontrolled, raging hormones on a teenager can cause as well as encourage them to want to touch the opposite sex or the same sex in some instances to seek gratification depending on how vicious the demon or spirit is trying to overwhelm them. People who cannot control those sexual urges can also become sexual predators all because they have to gratify that sexual desire. It is amazing that a lack of self-control over sexual urges can get you sexual assault charges and possibly heavy jail time.

We eventually found out this same teenager of mine at the time was getting into pornography himself. How we found out was that his behavior started to change. For starters, he began to spend way too much time in the bathroom and behind locked doors in general. In the mornings, he would take ridiculous amounts of time dressing for school. An alarm went off for me as a parent because it all seemed too familiar to me as a 13-year-old when I was exposed initially to pornography. These were the exact patterns I found myself following in order to entertain my addiction.

We begin to notice that he was more eager to get his hands on electronic devices (i.e., tablets, cell phones specifically) that he could easily take with him in private places without us noticing.

Our children had strict curfews that were always enforced. They were to be in bed by 9:00 p.m. on school nights. No tablets or any other electronics were to be played with. Because the oldest two were consistently on punishment because of bad behavior and poor grades in school, they were stripped of electronics quite often. Somehow at night when they were supposed to be asleep, they would be under the covers looking and playing with their tablets or whatever electronic device they had.

Quite a few times during those nights, we found out my oldest stepson was looking at pornographic websites. When we confiscated his electronic devices and looked in the history section, we found he had searched a plethora of various websites. His mother and I were concerned, and the first question we asked was how did he know about these sites. The next question we had was who was responsible for exposing him to the websites. As quiet as it was kept from my wife at the time, I was still into pornography and masturbation during my marriage. It was not until towards the end of our marriage that I made a conscious decision to be delivered. Most importantly I did not have DVDs or pornographic material lying around available to him. I kept my struggle as much of a mystery as I could. Therefore, it was not because of my negligence that he was exposed to pornography. When I was into pornography, it was always on my phone, and I never let my kids play on my phone. Plus I always had a code or pattern that had to be implemented to get into it.

After several conversations, it came out that it was his peers at school who exposed him to pornography. To my recollection from time to time, a few of his friends would look at pornographic websites on their tablets during school. Being curious and the social bug that he is, of course, he was going to look. The looking sparked his interest to want to see more. Therefore, when he got the opportunity, he would browse the web on his own to see more. In a sense, I am thankful that my stepson had his struggle with pornography, even though when I found out he was wrestling with it I felt responsible. I knew that I was bound for years and the damage a porn addiction can do spiritually, mentally, and emotionally to a person can be overwhelming.

Finding out about his struggle helped me make a sound decision to come out and be delivered myself so I could help him. I owed my stepson that much. The first solution to helping him was to be an example to him by first walking in my own deliverance, for real. My truth of my stepson having an addiction to porn is a perfect example that when you carelessly indulge in sin, if you do not seek help or deliverance, your own children will have to fight the same demons and generational or family curses. I knew that I would not be able to help him if I was still bound myself.

His mother was livid about his engaging in pornography. While I understood the severity of the addiction, I knew what I had to do to reach him, and that was to expose myself and tell him about my addiction. It meant me possibly feeling ashamed, dirty, and embarrassed, but I would rather feel those feelings than not save him from an unnecessary experience. His mother fussed, cussed, and yelled at him. All it did was cause him to shut down and not trust her to the point where he could be transparent enough to get any resolve from her. I told his mother that I would take care of this particular issue with him one-on-one. With her knowing about my struggle, she agreed and gave us privacy to talk.

I sat him down and told him that I understood and knew the struggle he was facing. He had a perplexed look on his face. I told him that I too used to be heavily into pornography and I explained to him how I became addicted, the struggle to get delivered, and the damage it did to my life. When I was honest with him, he opened up because for the first time his parent could relate to him. Once he was made aware of my experiences, he knew that whatever I had to say or advice I had to offer would be valuable. Surely enough, it had a strong chance of steering him in the right direction, because I knew what I was talking about when it came to addressing his struggle.

The conversation was long overdue. He opened up about a slew of stuff he was curious about, and we were able to address it. That particular conversation indeed brought us closer together. From that moment on anytime he had urges or the desire to sneak and browse the internet for pornography, or if something happened in school, whether it was an interaction he had with a female that triggered those urges he had, he came to me without hesitation. We would talk, and I would give him tips on how to channel his focus and energy when temptation came to overwhelm him.

It is vital for parents of teenagers to take the necessary precautions to not only reduce the likelihood of their teenagers becoming addicted to pornography but to reduce the likelihood of being exposed to pornography. The first step a parent should take is to begin to pay attention to what their children are exposed to. A parent must monitor what their child watches on television. While it may be a cliché, the phrase "sex sells" is indeed an accurate statement. Sex is advertised just about everywhere these days. Whether if it is in commercials, movies, TV series, on the side of buses, advertising billboards off of main streets and highways, it is everywhere! Even cartoons have sexually perverted references these days. The beautiful thing is that cable providers and even smart TV's give parents the option to put parental locks on various stations or movies that are rated R, XXX, or whatever the parent feels is inappropriate for their children. Therefore, if a child tries to watch a certain movie or network, they have to input a code. Parents, check with your cable provider and the user guide of your television devices on how to put parental codes to use.

The next step a parent can utilize is paying attention to the friends their children have as well as monitoring the conversations they have with those friends. The type of people your child hangs around says a great deal about your child, their interest, and possibly the type of behavior they exemplify when not in your presence. It is no secret, teenagers do not have innocent, clean conversations among themselves 100 percent of the time when they are not in the presence of their parents. However, pay attention to the slang they use or phrases they say that are unfamiliar to you because it may or may not have sexual references.

A majority of teenagers have cell phones and do a plethora of texting and engaging in online chats. The beautiful thing about this for parents is that the parents pay the phone bills for the most part. Therefore, you have the opportunity to go to your cell phone carrier and get copies of text messages. Or if you are the type of parent I am, take your child's cell phone and go through it. Find out who they are talking to and or texting. Read the text messages, and whatever concerns you find, you should address them, and then redirect your child accordingly.

The third tip is to check your child's social media accounts. This is not the 80s or 90s. Therefore, children and teenagers are not in the house talking on landline phones with the possibility of you eavesdropping on their conversations. Teenagers today do more communicating on social media (Facebook, Snap Chat, Instagram, YouTube, Twitter, etc.). Find out exactly what social media accounts your child has. Youths today are so bold with their sexual references, vulgar language, and sexual activity that they document and post it all on social media.

For parents with daughters, check to see if your daughter has twerk videos on YouTube or any other social media outlet. Does she have pictures revealing her buttocks and breast, making sexual gestures and gyration movements? For parents with sons, find out if he has pictures on social media showing his genitals. Check their in boxes on Facebook, the DM (direct message) on Instagram, and investigate who they are talking to, and if they are having inappropriate conversations with anyone. If your child is not properly educated, they can even face criminal charges for sexting or soliciting sexual images of themselves, which can be classified as sexual harassment depending on the state in which you reside.

Lastly, another tip for parents is to do random checks and searches in your child's bedroom, book bags, dressers, etc. My philosophy is, "You are a child living in my house. Therefore, you have no privacy, and no room is off limits, including the bedroom. The fact I pay bills and provide is all the warrant I need to conduct a search." Look under their beds and hidden places in their rooms. Find out if they are owners of pornographic material, sex toys, or sex contraceptives that you know you did not give them. This also helps you to have a reason to have those uncomfortable conversations with them about these touchy subjects. Nevertheless, the discussion(s) needs to be held with your children. It is best if the issues are nipped in the bud rather than later on in their latter years when they are too far gone and too deep into their indulgences in the addiction. Either you educate them or risk the world giving them the wrong information that has the potential of ultimately ruining their lives.

Chapter 9

Know Your Triggers

I always compare a person with an addiction to pornography to a person who is asthmatic. Asthma is not curable. A person can grow out of asthma, but there is no cure. In the wrong environment or atmosphere, asthmatics risk having triggers that will exacerbate their asthma and cause a severe asthma attack. For example, an asthmatic that is outside for too long during the summer in the humidity, outside during spring when the pollen count is high or in a room where it is dirty and filled with dust may have an asthma attack. Even though there is no cure for asthma, there are suppressants like inhalers (e.g., albuterol) that are quick relievers and or medications that must be taken at specific times of the day to keep asthma under control, thereby, reducing the likelihood of asthma attacks.

It is the same way with individuals who have an addiction to pornography. Those with porn addictions, who are in the wrong environments, can trigger the addiction which eventually causes them to relapse. For a porn addict, the wrong environments include strip clubs, being in a room with someone who is watching movies with explicit nude and or sexual content, or being around someone who is watching music videos with women twerking. All of these create environments that can trigger the addiction.

Like asthmatics, porn addicts have suppressants to help maintain the addiction and keep it in check. The reality of it all is that the urges to entertain and self-gratify will never go away. The sexual desires will be there. However, we have to assess the situation. Does it require a quick reliever? For a porn addict, a quick reliever can be simple things such as immediately leaving the room, changing the station on the television, going to the gym to burn the energy, or taking a cold shower, to name a few.

Take the precautions to keep the urges in control, thus reducing the chances of an easy trigger that could cause you to relapse. Those measures consist of staying away from strip clubs knowing you cannot handle the environment without the atmosphere triggering something within you. Have someone put parental locks on your internet and cable stations with a code you do not know. Therefore, in the future when you get desires to surf On Demand or the internet for pornography you will be unsuccessful in doing so. Another preventive measure, especially for believers, is consistent prayer and fasting with the purpose of taking designated as well as idle time and dedicating it to seeking the face of God. Consistently ask God to keep you focused and strong when the urges arise. Stay in the Word of God and hold dear to your spiritual convictions.

Throughout my struggle, specific things would trigger my urges that would tickle my sexual desires for self-gratification causing me to relapse and fall to masturbation. One thing I found that can be a dangerous trigger is social media. By social media, I am specifically referring to Instagram, Facebook, YouTube, and

World Star Hip Hop. On these various social media portals, any and everyone has access to upload nude, provocative, or sexual content that can help a porn addict reach self-gratification through masturbation.

There was a season when I would browse YouTube for various videos of full-figured women twerking in booty shorts. Twerk videos on YouTube can be as long as three to five minutes. There was no sex in the videos, just women gyrating their hips and buttocks which gave me mental images of me grinding or even having sex with the various women in the videos. I can remember saving various videos on my favorites. Therefore, when I was a kid, and no one was home, I could easily find them and have my sessions.

Then there is Instagram. This particular application is vicious because it works well when hashtags are used. For example, in the search box, I could type "#twerkvideos," and any video that has been uploaded to the application with that particularly related hashtag in the caption would pop up in the search results, making it easy for me to narrow down and find specific content. In my search, I would come across all kinds of beautiful, voluptuous, full-figured women who were strippers or porn stars and looked very pleasing to the eye when they twerked. At the time when I was married, I stopped watching porn for a while and resorted to Instagram because I felt as if trying to watch pornography and not get caught was too risky. Plus, Instagram videos only lasted approximately ten seconds for the most part. All it took was ten seconds to get aroused, allowing the video to loop quite a few times to enhance a quick orgasm. Not too much hardcore porn is exposed on Instagram. If pornography is found, it normally does not stay posted too long before it is removed. However, there are numerous twerk videos available on Instagram.

Facebook is the one social media outlet with which I have to be careful because I utilize it more than any other social media outlet, and not everyone who is my Facebook friend is pure and prudish in their posting content. The problem with Facebook is that on your timeline your friend's post (pictures or videos), whether they initially uploaded the content themselves or shared them from other people's posts, can find its way on your timeline. What ends up happening is that as you scroll down your timeline to see what your friends are posting, you can easily find pictures or videos of pornography. There were times when I was working towards coming out of my addiction where it may have been days or weeks of not looking at pornography or masturbating, and then I would be on my phone scrolling down my Facebook timeline and boom! One of my friends shared a video of a girl twerking, or a woman bent over being penetrated, and it would trigger me. I would be aroused; my mind would start imagining and before you know it, I would run off to a bathroom or a space secluded to myself to masturbate with the aid of the content I happened to come across.

Then there is a website called World Star Hip Hop. This particular site is not solely a pornographic site; however, if you type in the right keywords, you will find various types of videos of people having sex. When it comes to the sex videos found on this site, there is nothing scripted about the material. Everything posted is "as it happened." Some things are caught on tape and happened to be posted. Meanwhile, others knowingly record themselves having sex and post it without care or concern. Nevertheless, I found this site to be a trigger for me. Although I did not frequent this particular site much, it has the power to cause a porn addict to relapse.

Another trigger that is detrimental to a porn addict is late night TV programs (real sex, Cathouse, and other cable shows). These shows tend to come on after midnight. When I was young, they would come on HBO or Showtime network stations. The sex scenes are enticing, very dramatic, and stimulate the imagination. If you use them as an aid to masturbate, they bring it to life in a sense.

Then there are music videos or rap videos. Music videos are not as bad as the other triggers, but, they can trigger an addiction. Music videos can still be a threat to one who is seeking deliverance from masturbation. These days you have artists like Nicki Minaj, Beyoncé, or Rihanna, to name a few, who a lot of times appear in their videos half naked or have the camera emphasizing the enticing curves of their body shape. Then for women, you have male artists who are well-built, physically fit, and sometimes shirtless, grinding on the women in their videos. This can trigger something in the women who watch their videos.

I remember specifically when Nicki Minaj's video, *Anaconda*, was released I was drawn to it. I was never a Nicki Minaj fan prior to that video. However, from beginning to end, I was hooked. The twerking that the women were doing was quite enjoyable. For whatever reason, whenever Nicki would bend over, the camera angles made her look quite appetizing. I remember being married at the time and I was coming out of my addiction. I would be in the house, and I would sneak off to the bathroom to look at the video with the volume down. I never masturbated to the video, but I was always aroused. I had to make a decision that I would not relapse, so I forced myself to stop watching that particular video as well as others. A person who is battling a porn addiction must protect what they allow into their spirit by being cautious of what they hear and watch. As I stated earlier, when you see or expose yourself to certain things, it is hard to get rid of those mental images that have a way of always resurfacing in your mind and stirring up imagination and thoughts that can be hard to erase.

Another thing I noticed that can be a trigger is the basic attraction for the opposite sex, or for some attraction for the same-sex. What I mean by that is a man can go throughout his daily routine, walk down the street and see a fine woman standing at the bus stop. She could be a size 36-24-38, built like a brick house; and just her standing there looking attractive can trigger something. Men are visionaries by nature. Most men have the ability to undress a woman visually and see themselves in bed having sexual intercourse with them. The visual can be so real, it can cause him to entertain his dirty mind by having a masturbation session.

Women can see a man who is well-built and can undress him as well and trigger her hormones to go off. It is clear we will always find people attractive to the point where we can find ourselves so turned on by them and wanting to take them to bed. The key point to keep in mind is that the sin is not in the thoughts but in entertaining them. When we feed our desires the entrée of self-gratification, that is where the problem lies. We have to be disciplined enough to practice self-control and put under subjection thoughts and imagination(s) that can cause us to act outside of the will of God.

Lastly, a trigger for a porn addict can be as simple as reminiscing about past sexual encounters with former partners. A lot of times this happens when a person is bored, idle, and not productive. Being alone and not focused on the next phase of doing something constructive can get you in a heap of trouble. You could be doing something as simple as sitting at home and before you know it, you can randomly find yourself reminiscing about a sexual encounter you had with a former lover, the strangest place(s) in which you did them and how they rocked your world or turned you out, can trigger the desire to masturbate or want to look at pornography to put you in the mood and ultimately aid the masturbation session. No matter what the triggers are, know what your triggers are! Be mindful of them. Understand their power and that the devil can be crafty in utilizing them to cause you to either stay bound or relapse. Be vigilant, alert, and exemplify self-control.

Chapter 10

Preventing Relapse

Counterfeit deliverance will always come before true deliverance. What I mean by that is, when an addict with any kind of habit tries to become clean, they will have moments where they struggle to a place of full-fledged deliverance. The reality is not everyone can quit cold turkey on their addiction. A person has to first make up in their mind that they want to be delivered and then walk in their deliverance by creating the boundaries to help them throughout the process.

A person who struggles with an addiction or struggles with maintaining their deliverance does so because they have experienced periods of relapsing. Relapsing is simply the reoccurrence of a past condition. For example, a person may go days, weeks, or even a few short months without entertaining their addiction. They may have been clean for a short period. However, the deliverance is short lived because they were either around the person who encouraged them or they did not avoid triggers that caused the addiction; therefore, they relapsed.

For me, relapsing into my porn addiction was one of the worst experiences. I can remember countless times where I had periods where I stayed away from pornography and masturbation for days, weeks, sometimes months; and I remember feeling like I was on top of the world. I felt free, delivered, and no longer overtaken once and for all. But what I failed to understand is that the more I made an effort to be free, the harder the devil fought to ensure that I relapsed and make it seem as if I would never be free. Lust, pornography, and other sexual perversions are all spirits.

Luke 11:24-26 (NIV) says, *"When an impure spirit comes out of a person, it goes through arid places seeking rest and does not find it. Then it says, 'I will return to the house I left.' When it arrives, it finds the house swept clean and put in order. Then it goes and takes seven other spirits more wicked than itself, and they go in and live there. And the final condition of that person is worse than the first."* Every time a person experiences short-term deliverance, the spiritual rationale as to why they relapse is because the demonic forces work twice as hard with reinforcement to come on harder and stronger each and every time. The Gospel of Luke stated that once the spirit leaves the body, it comes back finding it clean and in order. When you work towards deliverance, the enemy does not like when you make conscious decisions to live holy and clean and when you make your flesh subject to the power of God. Spirits, whether godly or ungodly, need a body in which to manifest so they can function. When evil spirits come back with reinforcement, Scripture says that the final condition is worse than the first. I can remember each time I relapsed I felt worse and worse. I felt like filth, a dirty rag, a pervert. It was indeed an unpleasant feeling.

A great portion of the church has the view that there is no such thing as a deliverance process. The stance is that God delivers instantly and all people can go cold turkey. I have seen and heard of testimonies of people going to various deliverance services and people, through the power of God, have walked away once and for all at a moment's notice from their various addictions. However, that is not the case for everybody. The reality of addictions and for people who got addicted to various things is that it took time to become addicted to pornography or whatever the addiction is and sometimes it takes time to be fully delivered. Everyone's process to deliverance varies. God is a God of free will, choices, and decisions. For people who were strong enough to walk away from their addictions, either cold turkey or over a period, it had to have happened first by making a decision.

Joshua 24:15 (NIV) says, *"But if serving the Lord seems undesirable to you, then choose for yourselves this day whom you will serve."* One thing I love about God is He never forces Himself on us. He presents all He has to offer to us, and He leaves it up to us to make the decision to lay aside every weight and sin that so easily entangles us as stated in Hebrews 12:1. We have to choose to stop relapsing and going through the same cycle over and over again. For me, I grew tired of relapsing, playing with God, and playing with my deliverance. I grew tired of making a mockery of my walk with God. Although publicly no one knew of my struggles, it was the internal secret convictions I had that were troubling me. Lastly, I was tired of my hard work and progress going down the drain.

A continuous state of relapsing back into a pornography addiction does not have to be your reality. Weigh your options as well as your promises from God when you walk away from the desires of the flesh versus the few moments of self-gratification. Make the decision in terms of what is better for you: living to please God or yourself. For me, I did not want to lose my anointing, the presence of God, or my life for being disobedient. Make the decision.

Chapter 11

Being Delivered

Along with my personal story, we have spent a great deal of time in this book discovering what pornography is, the types of pornography, the causes and effects of a porn addiction, and the problems one encounters with an addiction to pornography. Now we must focus on what it takes to be delivered from a porn addiction, the sacrifices one must make to experience true deliverance. What is deliverance and how does the Word of God define it? Simply put, deliverance is when God sets a person free from evil spirits, bondage, habits, and or various lifestyles that offend Him and are contrary to the Biblical Canon.

Before we talk about the steps to deliverance and the tips on maintaining your deliverance, we must put to rest the misconceptions that hinder a person's deliverance. The first misconception is when an addict says to himself or herself, "It'll go away." An addiction to pornography is nothing to take lightly. It is not just a phase; it is a stronghold puppeteered by the hands of the demonic spirits of lust and perversion. It will not just go away. If it will just go away, then why are you still wrestling with the addiction, feeling guilty and overtaken by it? An addict must be aware that the reason why it will not just go away is that they are wrestling with a spirit. Ephesians 6:12 (KJV) declares, *"For we wrestle not against flesh and blood, but against principalities, against powers, against the rulers of the darkness of this world, against spiritual wickedness in high places."* The point is a porn addiction is nothing but spiritual warfare where the addiction itself is geared to self-gratification rather than seeking and pleasing God.

The second misconception is when a person says, "I can stop anytime I want to." Anytime an addict tells someone that they can stop anytime they want to they are trying to convince themselves that they are in control of their addiction when in actuality they know they are not. In the beginning, my problem was that I felt I could stop anytime I wanted to, but I was scared to admit that I had an addiction.

Then we have the problem of being in denial. The first pre-step to deliverance is admitting that you have a problem. A person who is in denial about their addiction hinders their deliverance process. Until a person admits that they have a problem and or that they have a porn addiction, they will forever be wrapped up, tangled up, and tied up to their bondage. Now let us go over some steps to take to experience true deliverance from an addiction to pornography.

Steps to Deliverance

1. Make up Your Mind

Romans 12:1-2 (NIV) says, *"Therefore, I urge you, brothers and sisters in view of God's mercy, to offer your bodies as a living sacrifice, holy and pleasing to God—this is your true and proper worship. Do not conform to the pattern of this world, but be transformed by the renewing of your mind. Then you will be able to test and approve what God's will is—His good, pleasing, and perfect will."*

The first step to deliverance from a porn addiction is to make up in your mind that you want something different. We have to acknowledge that we do not belong to ourselves and that God's design for any type of sexual gratification is through marriage. Paul, in Romans 12, gives us a charge to give our bodies back to God and submit to His will and His way. In return, He will provide ways to reward us that line up to His plan for our lives.

Paul goes on to say to not conform to this world. The world, carnal people, will convince us as believers that it is okay to lust after people and tickle the imagination of being intimate with them and simultaneously sexually gratify ourselves through masturbation. But we are not to compromise our beliefs or be complacent in our bondage. Paul then challenges us to be transformed by renewing our minds. The only way we can be changed and walk away from the bondage of a porn addiction is to make a decision to turn away from the lust of the flesh. Romans 12:1-2 is a call to spiritual maturity.

2. Confession

First John 1:9 (NIV) says, *"If we confess our sins, He is faithful and just and will forgive us our sins and purify us from all un-righteousness."* Never be ashamed to confess your dirtiest secrets to God. God knows all of our struggles. He is just waiting for us to admit our faults in return for His saving grace. It does not matter who we are. We can be the chiefest of sinners, but when we go to

God with a sincere heart, He is surely ready to purge us of the impurities and iniquities we allowed in our lives, therefore, forgiving us. But we have to come clean to God.

3. Repent

Acts 3:19 (NIV) says, *"Repent, then, and turn to God, so that your sins may be wiped out, that times of refreshing may come from the Lord."* After we confess our sins unto God that we have an addiction, we must repent and seek God for forgiveness of our disobedience of offending Him and living contrary to His Word. His Word promises to wipe out our sins. Even when people try to hold our mess over our head, the blessing is God will not.

Sin, once committed, is like a person who gets a tattoo. When a person gets a tattoo, no matter how much they try to use soap and water, the tattoo will not be removed. The only way a tattoo can be removed is through a surgical process. It is the same with sin. No matter how much you try, you cannot remove the stench of sin, consequences, guilt, or shame. Neither can you remove the memory and or the reality that it happened. In order to do that, one must allow God to conduct spiritual surgery to remove the evidence.

We must allow God room to remove the power of the mental images have that try to tempt us to indulge. We must give Him the room He needs to wipe our slate clean. When we give Him room to change our hearts and change our desires Paul said, He will refresh us. There is no feeling like the feeling when God refreshes your spirit, and you know for a fact that the struggles you used to have to tussle with in your mind, whether or not you were going to entertain it or not, are now no-brainers and easy to walk away from. When God refreshes your spirit and cleanse out your system, you are more alert and cautious as to what you entertain, even the addictions you used to succumb easily to because you know what it took to get delivered. Therefore, you do all you can to protect your deliverance and your walk with God.

4.   Turn Away

Second Chronicles 7:14 (NIV) says, "*If My people, who are called by My name, will humble themselves and pray and seek My face and turn from their wicked ways, then I will hear from heaven, and I will forgive their sin and will heal their land.*" Here even in the Old Testament, we see the writer telling Israel of God's plan to forgive their sins. Once they follow through with the instructions, God would bring healing unto the people. Once the people humbled themselves, prayed, and sought God, they were charged to turn from sin.

We have an obligation to turn away from the addiction to pornography each and every time we are confronted with falling back into the temptation of entertaining the lust of the flesh. Notice, the writer said forgiveness of sin came after Israel turned away from sin. When I stopped playing with God through what I called "Pitiful Repentance," then and only then was I forgiven truly by God. "Pitiful Repentance" is when you repent over and over, but shortly you find yourself right back in the same position sinning again. I kept telling God I was sorry, but He took my repentance as a joke because I was not serious about my deliverance. When

I was tired of my own self-inflicted cycle, I made up in my mind that enough was enough. I was ready to change, ready to experience God as the deliverer that I read about in the Bible. I was ready to put His delivering power to the test by letting Him free me from something I struggled with privately. I was ready to turn away, never to look back. Make a decision to turn away.

5. Recognize You Need God to Conquer Your Addiction

Romans 8:37 says, "*No, in all these things we are more than conquerors through Him who loves us.*" Even with an addiction to pornography, we have the ability to conquer the stronghold and be set free. God loves us so much that He gives us the power to overcome any obstacle, hindrance, or temptation. We must recognize that we need His Holy Spirit to help us say no, help us turn away, and stay away from the addiction to pornography. Acquiring deliverance, being delivered, or even maintaining deliverance is never of one's own power or might but by the power of God.

6. Recognize You Can Do It!!

Philippians 4:13 says, "*I can do all things through Christ that gives me strength to do so.*" When I was coming out of my addiction, one of the questions I asked myself and God was, "Can I really walk away and stay away?" God took me back to this Scripture to remind me where my capability, strength, and endurance resided in order for me to walk in my deliverance once and for all. It all resided in Christ. However, I had to do my part and apply the Word of God to my life. Understand and grasp that it will not be easy to be delivered and maintain deliverance, but God will give you what you need to prevail.

7. Seek Counseling, Therapy if Necessary

Proverbs 15:22 says, *"Plans fail for lack of counseling, but with many advisers they succeed."* If you are reading this book, it is a sign you are seeking information for yourself or someone you know about how to be delivered from an addiction to pornography. Without a plan or putting the proper precautions in place and seeking help, the plan to be and stay delivered will fail. One must be willing to seek help, if necessary, even if that means visiting a therapist or counselor. Their job is to help you put treatment plans in motion to aid your progression and hold you accountable. Counselors and therapists are trained to counsel and treat you from an unbiased viewpoint. The good thing about counselors and therapists is that they must protect your privacy and keep your conversations confidential. Therefore, you will not have to worry about your struggles to go public. If it does, and it is at their negligence, they can lose their license. Not only that, they really have no interests in putting your addictions on blast.

Tips on Maintaining Your Deliverance

The first tip in maintaining your deliverance from a porn addiction is to not be naïve and understand you will have temptation, moments where you want to relapse. You will have flashbacks and even desires. However, it is the enemy trying to entice you back to a life or a habit that once had you bound.

The second tip is that when desires come on strong, know that it is time to initiate self-control and resist the spirits of lust and perversion. James 4:7 (NIV) says, *"Submit yourselves, then, to God. Resist the devil, and he will flee from you."* The truth is implementing this Scripture is easier said than done. The devil is cunning and manipulative, and he comes on strong. It is never easy to resist his devices because he never tempts us with things we do not find enticing and unattractive. He comes to us with things that grab our undivided attention. We have to exemplify discipline to resist the devil and his tactics by turning away each and every time he tries to overwhelm us.

The third tip in maintaining your deliverance is to always understand that the operator behind an overwhelming porn addiction is a spirit. It is a demonic spirit of lust and perversion that has no barrier on age, gender, or race. That is why children as young as twelve and thirteen years old become addicted. The spirits of lust and perversion have no age bracket. No one is exempt from the possibility of being vulnerable, overtaken, or bound.

The fourth tip is to be sensitive to know what your triggers are. We talked earlier about triggers. When you know what your triggers are and the potential they have to cause you to relapse into the addiction, it helps you to put measures in place. For example, if you know that twerk videos can distract you and cause you to falter, then stay off Instagram, Facebook, YouTube, and other social media outlets. Stay out of strip clubs if you know that environment triggers your addiction. If certain movies that have sex scenes trigger the addiction, then stop watching them. Know the specific things you watch and hear that can trigger your addiction and cause it to resurface.

The fifth tip is to practice discipline and self-control. First Corinthians 9:27 says, *"No, I strike a blow to my body and make it my slave so that after I have preached to others, I myself will not be disqualified for the prize."* I heard one of my spiritual uncles, Bishop Bryant Martin, say one time, "One of the major components of holiness is discipline." The only way deliverance will be maintained is that you have to upkeep it with discipline. Understand you will not be able to control your environment 24/7. You may be at family functions or around people and or in someone's home where they may have sexual conversations, or pornographic material (magazines, etc.) lying around their house. They may even cut on a pornographic flick while you are in their home or have it on an electronic device and you may happen to walk by them and look over their shoulders while they are watching it. You have to be disciplined enough to not let it trigger you. If you are not strong enough, then excuse yourself from their company because you know your deliverance is depending on it!

The sixth tip is to stay in consistent prayer, fasting, and seeking God. When you stay in the presence of God, it is hard to be a successful, comfortable heathen. When you continuously stay before God and make Him a priority, it becomes hard to find time to entertain the lust of the flesh.

The seventh tip is to get rid of all materials. Any magazines, DVD's, tapes, toys, or whatever you have that can lead to self-inflicted temptation, get rid of it. When you still have access to the materials, they consistently remind and tempt you to stay addicted or encourage periods of relapsing. Clean out your search history in your electronic devices; this helps as well.

The eighth tip is to understand that in most cases the change will not happen overnight. It is a process to deliverance. It took a while to become addicted. Therefore, it can take a while to get it out of your system. Seek counseling or therapy to help aid with the process to bring a level of accountability and to provide you with a plan of progress by which you can measure your deliverance.

The ninth tip is to change your company. First Corinthians 15:33 says, *Do not be misled: "Bad company corrupts good character."* You will never be able to reach true deliverance or maintain your deliverance if you are still hanging around the same people who have the same struggle as you. Those people will always make you feel comfortable about your sin or addiction. Hang around people who will hold you accountable, who are stronger than you that will empower you to want to stay delivered.

I have two allergies—all types of peanuts and shellfish. Some people are so badly allergic to peanuts and shellfish that they cannot be in the same room with them, because the smell alone will ignite an allergic reaction and, in some instances, they will break out. Others who are allergic can be around it and can take the smell, but if they touch or consume it, then they will surely have an allergic reaction. When you get delivered from an addiction to pornography, you must become spiritually allergic to the addiction. When you first become delivered, your spiritual allergic reaction must be so sensitive that being around conversations, strip clubs, movies, websites, or whatever triggers you have, will give you an immediate reaction. Therefore, you must stay away from it and be able to smell the triggers a mile away and stay out of the way.

When you mature in your deliverance, you gain strength that is out of this world. You can be around people who are having perverted conversations, drive past a strip club, see something on social media, flip through the television stations and see a movie that is in the middle of a sex scene and not be affected as long as you do not entertain it. Do not give the piqued interest an opportunity to let the spiritual allergy (addiction) flare up and cause you to have a reaction (relapse). In my personal experience, I am now strong enough that twerk videos do not easily affect me like they did before. However, if I keep my eyes on them long enough and try to find more videos, then I am allowing myself to be consumed, risking a homicidal spiritual death.

Lastly, the tenth tip is for those who are married. You play a vital role in your spouse's deliverance. Be willing to ensure that you and your body are available to help release intimacy among each other. Do not be afraid to spark things up in your bedroom, making your spouse feel as if it is pointless to watch porn and masturbate because you can satisfy them sexually in ways that the addiction cannot. Not only that, but let your spouse know that you bring another level of intimacy and genuine love that they will never find through a porn addiction. Be sensitive and understand that they are struggling to try to break free from a powerful addiction. Spend time together, pray together, and be transparent. Allow your spouse to be transparent with you where they are comfortable to come to you to say, "Honey, I am tempted to watch porn." Rather than making them feel bad or judge them, take the time and energy to go handle your business in the marriage bed. Most of all, be patient because deliverance can be a process.

Chapter 12

Final Thoughts

No matter where a person is in their walk with the Most High, the Christian life is an ongoing journey. The goal of a believer is to strive every day to live according to God's Word and in compliance with the standard that He has set as it relates to Christian living. In 2 Corinthians 6:14-18, Paul gives a warning against idolatry. In verse 17 he charges believers to *come out from among them* (unbelievers) and *be separate thus says the Lord*. Regardless if one is addicted to pornography, masturbation or whatever addiction, God is calling us out of the overwhelming bondage it forces on the addict. Anything that a person devotes more time, energy, finances, and allegiance to than the Most High God has become their idol (god).

First Peter 5:8 (NIV) says, *"Be alert and of sober mind. Your enemy the devil prowls around like a roaring lion looking for someone to devour."* We as believers cannot be alert, sober, and sensitive to spiritual matters if we are overtaken by any type of addiction. When addictions plague us, it blinds us from seeing the reality that the enemy is devouring us by bondage, which is the by-product of entertaining and being intimate with the addiction. When we read verse 18 of 2 Corinthians, Chapter 6, the Lord tells us when we stay away from idolatry, He will be our Father, and we will be His sons and daughters. Then, what I love about it is right after verse 18, Paul immediately goes into 2 Corinthians 7:1 (NIV) and says, *"Therefore, since we have these promises, dear friends, let us purify ourselves from everything that contaminates body and spirit, perfecting holiness out of reverence for God."* We have God's promise (His Word) that when we put Him first and put away self-gratification; i.e., purify ourselves of any person, habit, addiction, etc. that we placed in front of God, we will have a covenant of sonship with Him that is beyond our imagination.

We have a duty to perfect ourselves. Notice Paul did not say *BE* perfect but simply PERFECT holiness. It is something one must keep in continuous action. We should never get to a place of self-righteousness, thinking we have arrived and that we are above temptation and addictions and that we are untouchable from the pressures of humanity. Because as soon as we think we are untouchable, life, trouble, trials, adversity, temptation, and addiction will hit us like a bag of rocks. Sometimes when we are self-righteous and because we can easily sin as the next person, God will allow addictions(s) into our lives to humble us and remind us that it is not of our own might that we are holy, but it is through Him. Matthew 23:12 (NIV) says, *"For those who exalt themselves will be humbled, and those who humble themselves will be exalted."* Either you put yourself in check and place your flesh under subjection to the will of God, humbling yourself graciously by choice, or put God in a posture to where He has to rattle your life with strongholds to teach you humility. It will not be pleasant.

We all have a testimony. We all have a story of something we were entangled in from which God had to free us. Never be ashamed of your story no matter how ugly or embarrassing it is.

Final Thoughts

The problem is that we put too many filters on our testimony. We like to clean it up too much. However, when we filter it, we lose touch with the people God put in our path to reach because they cannot identify with us because even our flaws are too perfect. We as believers must learn to articulate the ugly part of our testimony so that we can help prevent someone from going down the same road we went down. Then we can help them enjoy the beauty of the life God designed for them.

When the Lord delivered me from pornography and mastur-bation, it became my duty to talk about my struggles because I owed it to that teen to give him the wisdom I wished someone had given me. I owe it to that married spouse that brought the addiction into their marriage. I owe it to the person who has low self-esteem and feels as if the only way they will be loved is through imaginational lust.

Many believers that belong to different sects of Christianity and different walks of life may condemn me because they find it hard to believe that I, a preacher, had such a struggle. But they are not my concern because they did not set me free or deliver me. Nor were they around to minister to me at the time where it was most critical. My mission, my call, along with the purpose of this book is to expose that God is real. He is a strong deliverer. God can clean you up and take the taste of sin out of your mouth. I must tell the world my unfiltered story. Revelations 12:11 says, "And *they overcame him by the blood of the Lamb and by the word of their testimony, and they did not love their lives to the death*." It is by Jesus' blood that we overcome addiction, and it is our duty to be witnesses of His delivering power and be willing to put ourselves on the line to defend His Gospel. John 8:36 says, *"Therefore if the Son makes you free, you shall be free indeed."* Make a choice to be healed, delivered, set free, and walk in your deliverance.

Contact Information

The author is available for book signings, poetry readings, book reviews, book club discussions, and other speaking opportunities.

You may contact him by writing to:

D'onte J. Carroll
Kingdom Living Publishing
P.O. Box 660
Accokeek, MD 20607

You may also send him an email at:
carrolldonte@yahoo.com

Connect with him on Facebook at
https://www.facebook.com/dontejcarroll

Or on Twitter at:
www.twitter.com/DonteJCarroll

This book and all other Kingdom Living Publishing (KLP) books are available at bookstores and distributors worldwide or from KLP.

Kingdom Living Publishing
P.O. Box 660
Accokeek, MD 20607
publish@kingdomlivingbooks.com
(301) 292-9010

www.ingramcontent.com/pod-product-compliance
Lightning Source LLC
Chambersburg PA
CBHW062002040426
42447CB00010B/1877